THE TRUE STORY OF
SKODA

DAVE RANDLE

SUTTON PUBLISHING

First Published in 2002 by
Sutton Publishing Limited · Phoenix Mill
Thrupp · Stroud · Gloucestershire ·GL5 2BU

British Library Cataloguing in Publication Data
A catalogue record for this book is available from the British Library

ISBN 0 7509 2565 5

> *This book is dedicated to my father,*
> *RON RANDLE,*
> *who inspired my lifelong passion for motoring*
> *and the motor car.*

Typeset in 10.5/13.5 Photina
Typesetting and origination by
Sutton Publishing Limited.
Printed in Great Britain by
J.H. Haynes & Co. Ltd, Sparkford.

CONTENTS

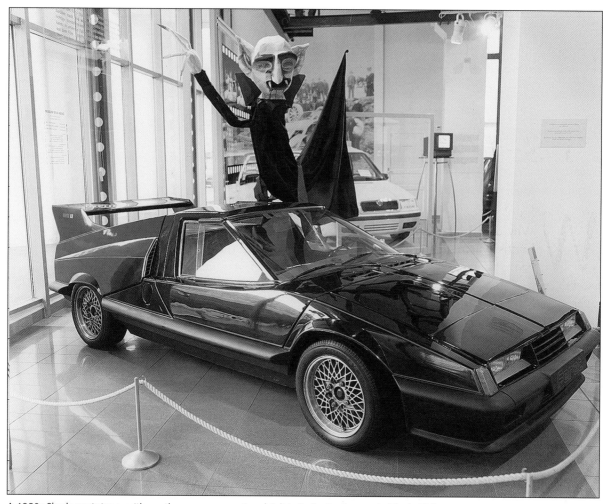

A 1980s Skoda prototype, with a rather more conventional Felicia in the background. (Skoda UK)

I SAY, I SAY, I SAY

What do you call a Skoda with twin exhausts? A wheelbarrow. Why does a Skoda have a heated rear window? To keep your hands warm while you're pushing it. Jokes like these have been doing the rounds for decades. Their perceived impact on Skoda's image has been strong enough for the company to launch reverse-psychology advertising campaigns in recent years. It would be difficult to determine to what degree Skoda owners from different eras would go along with the underlying sentiments, but this kind of humour very quickly acquires a life of its own, and most, if not all, 'Skoda jokes' have been applied to other marques – notably Lada, Yugo and Trabant.

Everyone likes a good joke, and a vocal majority never seems to tire of even the most ancient and familiar examples of the genre. The sea-change that has taken place in the firm's products has done nothing to diminish its light entertainment value, suggesting that, if Skoda hadn't existed, it would have been necessary to invent it

What do you call a Skoda with an open top? A skip. You have to laugh. But surely now the smile is wearing a little thin.

No one still tells jokes about the Edsel. And, in Germany, they used to say: 'Since only tin and paint is used, the Hanomag is soon produced' – demonstrating, it must be said, a remarkable facility for English verse – but you take the point. Who remembers the Edsel and who ever heard of the Hanomag?

Skoda is still very much with us. Over a hundred years on from its beginnings it has a sound identity, in the midst of a global industry changed out of all recognition, which puts it in a uniquely strong position to meet the powerful challenges that face all motor manufacturers in the coming years.

A good joke is one that has truth in it. The truth about the people at Skoda is that they've had their share of misery, but now they're laughing. The time for laughing at them is past. The moment has come to laugh with them.

CHRONOLOGY

1839	19 November	Emil Skoda born at Cheb.
1859		Count Arnost Waldstein begins building the Pilsen Machinery Works.
1865	27 September	Vaclav Laurin born.
1868	16 October	Vaclav Klement born.
1869		Emil Skoda buys Pilsen factory from Waldstein.
1876		Skoda begins to set up domestic and foreign sales offices.
1879		Otto Hieronimus born in Cologne.
1880		First cycling club in Central Europe founded in Prague.
1895	30 September	Laurin and Klement submit application to the town council of Mlada Boleslav for a permit to build a machine shop.
	December	They begin operations, with two workers and one apprentice, on pedal-driven machine tools.
1896		Klement writes and publishes the *Handbook for Cyclists and for those who wish to become them.*
	December	Company officially registered. Laurin and Klement now has twelve employees.
1897		Laurin declines position as President of the Jizera River Basin Chapter of the Czech Velocipedists' Club.
1898	February	Laurin & Klement receive permit to build a new factory.
1899		Skoda company goes public.
1900	8 August	Sir Emil Skoda dies on a train passing through Selzthal. Skoda turbines installed at Niagara Falls.
1905		Laurin & Klement now employ 355 workers and 170 machine tools.
	8 March	Bicycle manufacture ceases.
	April	Prague Automotive Show, prototype voiturette.
1907	1 January	Laurin & Klement embark on the establishment of a joint-stock (sharehold) company. Otto Hieronimus joins factory as competition driver – second best paid employee after Klement.
1908	8 January	First example HOP bus for Prague (HOP = Heavy Omnibus Prague), sold to the electric company for initial trials.
	7 March	Inauguration of regular bus service in Prague.
1909		Last four cylinder CCCC motorcycle.
1910		Motorcycle production ceases. Slavia name discontinued.
1911		Klement recognises need for a cheap 'people's car' and fears swamping by American Ford Model T. April launch of type S.
1913		Electric headlights begin to replace acetylene. Chain drive abandoned.
1918		End of war. Schneider buys 43,000 shares in Skoda.
1920		Laurin and Klement return to racing. First post-war motor show in Prague.
1922	May	Death of Otto Hieronimus.

1923	15 December	Skoda trademarks registered.
1925		S-type ceases production – Laurin and Klement's most successful line. Skoda merges with Laurin and Klement.
	27 June	Skoda Syndicate becomes 100 per cent owner of Mlada Boleslav plant.
	31 December	Sales network passes from Laurin and Klement to Skoda. Klement leaves.
1926		Laurin leaves company.
1927	4 December	Death of Count Alexander Kolowrat.
1928		Laurin in ill health.
1929		Wall Street Crash.
1930	3 December	Laurin dies of intestinal cancer in Prague.
1938	13 August	Death of Klement.
1939		War and German occupation.
1945	9 May	War ends. Luftwaffe bombs Mlada Boleslav.
1954		Devaluation.
1961	summer	Skoda Octavia imported to UK.
1963		1200 cc versions of Octavia and Felicia available.
1964		1000MB launched.
1969		100L and 110L launched.
1970		110R Coupé on sale in Europe.
1972		UK launch of 110R Coupé.
1976	autumn	Estelle previewed for UK market.
1977	spring	Estelle on sale in UK.
1978	April	Extensive revisions to Estelle answer early criticisms.

Outside the Skoda Museum at Mlada Boleslav. (Skoda UK)

1981	Rapid goes on sale.
1984	Further revisions to produce Estelle Series II.
1987	Arrival of the front-wheel-drive Favorit.
1991	Skoda joins Volkswagen Group.
1994	Felicia launched.
1995	Felicia goes on sale in UK.
1996	Launch of new Octavia.
2000	Fabia launched.
2001	New flagship model revealed at Geneva, revives 'Superb' name.

TIME AND PLACE

Skoda is one of the oldest surviving car marques. It had its origins in another century, in a time and place very different from our own. Its creators inhabited a cultural and political milieu that was singular in its own time and very far removed from the experience of the modern observer.

In order to see the subjects of this book in their true colour, therefore, we must sketch in a backdrop of the undulating fertile farming land of Bohemia; of ancient woodlands, by turns dark and impenetrable, or blazing with greens and reds that rival New England. A land of spectacular brooding castles, graceful palaces and labyrinthine timbered inns, its countryside watered by tributaries of the great Danube – known locally as the Moldava.

Its position at the heart of Central Europe has kept Bohemia high on the acquisition list of generations of disparate empire builders, and the development of the original Kingdom of Bohemia, comprising the Margravate of Moravia and Slovakia, was arrested first in the sixteenth century, when the Hungarian Hapsburg rulers were driven into exile by invading Turks. The Moravians knew an aristo when they saw one, so welcomed them, giving them the run of what is now the Slovakian capital, Bratislava, in return for which the new royals gave them little trouble. Hapsburg monarchs continued to be crowned at Bratislava for the next hundred years.

The Bohemian nobles were less taken with the idea. Rightly suspecting that their future was now firmly behind them, they tested the might of their oppressors in worthy but ill-founded military actions. They won a few battles, but convincingly lost the war when the Margravate was abolished and its territories turned into a suburb of Austrian Silesia. Not only were the nobles dispossessed, but many Czech political advances, including the religious reformation, were reversed.

However, Queen Maria-Theresa was not a despotic ruler by any means. Both she and her son, Joseph II, introduced their own reforms that ultimately shaped the Czech and Slovak Republics of today and, in their time, advanced the cause of the average citizen somewhat further than the nobles had had in mind. They it was who would initiate the move from feudalism to meritocracy and the democratisation of education; they who would foster Bohemia's participation in the industrial revolution.

But in 1741, before many of their reforms could be implemented, in a pointedly unholy alliance with the huffy ex-nobles, Holy Roman Emperor

Prague today is the capital of a thriving independent state. (Author)

Frederick of Prussia turned up, with the Dukes of Saxony and Bavaria. As the Queen exited stage left, the nobles proclaimed the latter Duke, Charles Albert, King of Bohemia.

It was now Maria-Theresa's turn to get stroppy and she saw to it that Charles Albert was not long to reign over them, by systematically retaking the kingdom over the following months for the Hapsburgs. Although forced to cede the majority of the newly industrialised areas to Prussia, she was recrowned Queen in Prague in 1743.

After this phantom renaissance, the Bohemian Kingdom faded away, its territories becoming provinces of an increasingly centralised and bureaucratic Austria. The Czech nobles were stripped, once more, of their positions of power, to be replaced by faceless imperial employees. German became the official language.

Following Maria-Theresa's death in 1790, Joseph II continued the pattern of what might be called enlightened suppression. His 1781 Edict of Toleration even gave citizens the freedom to practise unorthodox religions, but his underlying philosophy of Germanisation further eroded the identity and integrity of the kingdom. None the less his social and educational reforms paved the way for undreamt of socio-economic improvement.

Stripped of its feudal power, the nobility turned its attention to fledgling industrial developments. By leasing parts of their estates to glass and coal enterprises, they could provide themselves with the money and position denied them by the state.

By the end of the eighteenth century, there were schools and colleges for the peasantry and the population was booming. Despite the efforts of Joseph's successor, Leopold II, to appease the nobles on his accession in 1790, his two year reign was not long enough to interrupt the tide of progress. By now there was a growing Czech intelligentsia and they, rather than the distracted nobles, would guide the future destiny of the country.

Under Francis II a national revival took place. A chair for the Czech language was founded at Charles Ferdinand University in 1791 and professors Dobrovsky and Jungmann assembled a literary language from the vestiges of peasant patois and shared Slavic roots, while Jesuit priest Anton Bernovak developed the Slovakian language from surviving dialects there.

Serfdom was finally abolished as late as 1848 and Frantisek Palacky's *History of the Czech People* provided a focus for burgeoning nationalism, resulting in a series of revolutions in that year. But the country was to remain under foreign control for another sixty years, ruled over by a succession of representatives of the newly aligned Austro-Hungarian Empire.

Despite continuing nationalistic friction, though, substantial concessions were made by the imposed power. The Language Decree of 1880 put Czech on an equal footing with German in matters of administration and law within Bohemia's borders, and in 1882 the

Master, at last, of its own destiny, the city is still coming to terms with the enormity of its new-found responsibility. (Author)

Charles Ferdinand University was divided into two faculties – one German as before, the other Czech-based.

In 1900 university professor Tomas Masaryk founded the Czech Progressive Party. As a combined result of continued internal struggle and the sweeping changes brought about on the international stage by the First World War a newly, and wholly, independent Czechoslovakia came into being on 28 October 1918, and Masaryk was elected its first president.

The early years of the Skoda story overlap the final decades of these political events and developments. History was to deliver another lifetime of interruption with the death blow inflicted on the independent state in 1939, but that is for a later chapter.

To the firm's founding fathers, growing up in the latter part of the nineteenth century, everything was achievable and the only way was up.

After centuries of repression, the streets, squares, bridges and gardens buzz and crackle with rediscovered pride and energy. In less than a decade Prague has transformed itself from soul-starved outpost into the epicentre of Europe's cultural and spiritual resurgence. (Author)

THE MEN BEHIND THE MARQUE

EMIL SKODA

Despite his seniority in terms of age, and the fact that it's his name that goes on the cars, Emil Skoda doesn't really enter the story until quite late in the day. Born in the once great fortified city of Cheb on 19 November 1839, Skoda was educated at the Czech Technical College before going on to receive specialist training at Karlsruhe and Stuttgart. He worked for a time in Chemnitz and Magdeburg, where he demonstrated such precocious managerial skills and innate understanding of industrialism's emerging possibilities that he was put in charge of Count Arnost Waldstein's Pilsen Machine Works at the tender age of twenty-seven.

Like a number of his fellow nobles, Waldstein fancied a piece of the industrial future, so had shrewdly bought a load of machinery from a firm that had gone into liquidation. With a combination of megalomaniac vision and a more realistic need to house his knockdown purchases, he had constructed a huge machine shop and factory complex, which he staffed with over a hundred employees.

On Skoda's arrival in 1866, with the commercial world shell-shocked by fallout from the Franco-Prussian War, Waldstein's chimneys were guttering and his staff down to forty-odd souls. If Skoda was such a bigshot ideas-man, let him get the Count out of this one. And get him out of it he did, literally, a mere three years on, when he bought the whole works for himself.

Where the Count had been using his machines to produce other machines for people who had no use for them, Skoda turned the place over to the production of the common denominator of industrial progress, steel. Everyone from boltmakers to shipbuilders needed iron and steel – and the more refined and less raw the raw material, the better.

Emil Skoda (1839–1900). (Skoda UK)

Skoda fired up his first foundry in 1871, and every blast from his steam-driven bellows fed more energy into his manifold expansion. He matched it, not only as an able administrator, engineer and troubleshooter, but also as an energetic self-publicist, promoting his products, and his name, far beyond the borders of Bohemia, and even the Empire.

By the late 1880s things were going great guns – again, literally – as Skoda's pioneering experiments in armour-plating led to the development in Pilsen of the world's first 150mm field cannon. Soon established in the front rank of armaments manufacturers, Skoda, none the less, believed in diversification, and continued to produce steel and steam engines for industry to back up the surefire success of the ordnance division.

In 1900 the company was expanding on all fronts. Skoda turbines had just been installed at the Niagara Falls in Canada and Skoda himself had been elevated to Bohemia's House of Lords when, on 8 August, he died in a railway carriage as his train was passing through Selzthal.

By this time the company had a momentum of its own. Skoda's personality and business style was stamped upon it in perpetuity. If he had gone, his spirit lived on in the enterprise along with his name.

Like Krupps and Vickers, Skoda experienced something of a bonanza because of the chance outbreak of the First World War. But if it seemed as if it was all going its way for the duration, the good news of the founding of the Czechoslovak Republic in 1918 masked the fact that its biggest (indeed, its only major) client, the Austrian Empire, had itself gone into liquidation. There was no compensation scheme in those days. Unpaid invoices would remain unpaid. Through no fault of its own the Pilsen Works was in serious trouble.

But it had been in trouble before, and Skoda had got it out. The new board of directors set about doing so again by taking Skoda's well-earned reputation to someone else who understood the business they were in. The vision and the confidence to seek support abroad were not commonplace attributes at the beginning of the twentieth century. They are not that at the beginning of the twenty-first. But, like their founder, the Skoda board had no thought of failure. They approached the French armaments giant, Schneider, and succeeded in selling them a 60 per cent stake in the company. On the strength of that, a leading Czech bank, Zivnobanka, provided the remaining financial support to get the company producing and profitable again. This was soon achieved, and the Pilsen Works was active on numerous levels, absorbing other established companies and re-establishing its position as a jewel in the Republic's industrial crown.

Skoda's first automotive venture involved building France's Hispano-Suiza prestige cars under licence. Czechoslovak competitors were building home-grown cars by this time, but Pilsen stuck with assembly, not only of cars but also Sentinel steam lorries from Britain.

The Automobile Division at Pilsen was established in 1919 and, in addition to the Hispano-Suizas and now petrol versions of the Sentinel, began to produce its own engines, military vehicles and tractors.

But the genuine Skoda car owes its origins to the acquisition, in June 1925, of the firm of Laurin & Klement.

VACLAV LAURIN

Count Arnost Waldstein was already making plans to put Emil Skoda in charge of his Pilsen operation when Vaclav Laurin was born, on 27 September 1865, in a suburb of Turnov. No one would have connected the two events. It was unlikely, to say the least, that the lives of the multi-talented, upwardly mobile business magnate and this child of poverty-stricken farm labourers would be united by a common thread. Neighbours and fellow workers of his parents, Vaclav senior and Marie, expected them to set the child to work on the farm, as soon as he was able, as they and their parents had done. But the Laurins intended to break the circle. They could see the world was changing. Even in their own misery, they could hope for better things for their evidently talented son, so succeeded in securing him an apprenticeship with a fitter in Turnov, as soon as he was old enough to be away from home.

On completing his apprenticeship in 1880, young Vaclav enrolled in the college of artisans in Mlada Boleslav. Graduating three years later, he spent some time working for a master-locksmith by the name of Jan Najman, but was not yet ready to settle. For a dozen or more years he moved from job to job, town to town, even country to country, increasing his store of knowledge and further honing his own engineering skills.

Records of his movements in this period are vague, but it is known that he presented himself before an examining board in Dresden in 1893, who pronounced him qualified to service steam engines, and that shortly after this he returned to Turnov. Here he went into partnership with a bicycle maker called Kraus. Evidently he had made a crown or two on his travels and was shrewd enough to know the bicycle was the coming thing.

Throughout his life Laurin remained something of an enigma. Self-deprecating and modest in the extreme, he none the less conducted his life and career with great singlemindedness and no small success. In 1894, at the age of twenty-nine, he married crofter's daughter Emilie Beranova.

Things were jogging along at Turnov until Kraus came into some money of his own, whereupon Laurin's role changed from facilitator to meddler, and the atmosphere turned frosty. By this time, though, Laurin knew all he needed to know about bicycles to go and set up somewhere else.

With the proceeds from Turnov and the repaid investment money, he set the family up in a house in Mlada Boleslav, having first ensured there was no existing cycle enterprise in the town. But as he continued to research potential sites and collaborators, disturbing rumours began to reach him of another individual with similar plans to his own.

Vaclav Laurin (1865–1930). (Skoda UK)

What if, just as his plans were realised, the man Klement set up in opposition to him in Mlada Boleslav? This town wasn't big enough for the both of them.

VACLAV KLEMENT

In October 1868 when Vaclav Klement was born, Laurin had just passed his third birthday and, one month off thirty, Skoda was making plans to buy the Pilsen plant from Waldstein. Having himself made the break from farm labouring, Vaclav's father, Josef Klement would have had high hopes for his new son, though he might have viewed a future in the motor industry with mixed feelings in his own new career as a postilion. Like Laurin's parents, Josef and his wife, Anna, had been born with no advantages. Serfdom may have been abolished on the statute books, but working on the land for a pittance continued to be the accepted way of keeping body and soul together, at least until the newly educated generations took over.

By the time Vaclav was ten years old his mother had died and Josef had married again. His stepmother was less interested in his intellectual advancement than his immediate wage-earning potential, so volunteered him to herd cattle for the local blacksmith. Fortunately his schoolteacher, Mr Ctibor, took a more altruistic view and arranged an apprenticeship for him with a bookseller in Slany.

Nothing could be much further removed from the company of cows than life at Mr Vokoun's bookshop, with the possible exception of the sleeping arrangements. These consisted of a heavy wooden bed that had to be manhandled into place each night. Since Vaclav was required to occupy it in the foyer of the shop, it also had to be removed each morning to make way for the customers.

The luxuriantly bearded, cigar-smoking bookseller was a genuine intellectual and attracted others of his kind to his apartments, busting Vaclav's mind wide open to new ideas and ways of thinking. Among the visitors was Vilem Michl, a farm-machinery manufacturer who had diversified into bicycles. His 'Admirable' Velocipedes were part of a revolution in which the possibility of private transport was conceivable, for the first time ever, for those without land or stables. Taking advantage of his acquaintance, the young apprentice would take every opportunity to hire one of Michl's boneshakers and familiarise himself with the new technology.

When he was in a position to do so, Klement arranged to continue his education at night school, and at the end of four years with Volkoun was sufficiently qualified to take a position with Valecka in Prague, the city's leading booksellers. Here, the importance of the bicycle was even more manifest. The first cycling club in Europe had been founded in Prague in 1880 at the CKV Smichov factory.

Most eighteen-year-olds would have been more than happy to have a well-paid and respected job at the centre of national fashion and power. Not Klement. When, after only a year in Prague, he heard of a

Vaclav Klement (1868–1938).
(Skoda UK)

management vacancy in Mlada Boleslav, he astonished his colleagues by going after it. Novotny's in Zelezna Street sold not only books but also musical instruments and sheet music, and operated as a lending library. Klement passed the interview without difficulty and his continued social rise seemed inexorable. He bought his own cycle and founded Mlada Boleslav's first cycling club.

Meanwhile, his commercial success was such that he was able to buy the business from Jan Novotny on 27 July 1891. At the age of twenty-three he was running his own business, though it would take him another three years to pay for it. That didn't stop him from applying to the authorities for a licence to sell cycles. Klement knew that Laurin and Josef Kraus were assembling and repairing bicycles in nearby Turnov, but, thanks to the club, his own shop had already become a centre for Mlada Boleslav's cyclists. In addition to the leading Czech magazine, *Cyklista*, he stocked import titles that were devoured with similar enthusiasm by the cognoscenti.

On 2 June 1894 he married Antonie, the nineteen-year-old daughter of a shopkeeper from Liblice. Increasingly she took responsibility for the running of the shop, while Vaclav concentrated his attentions ever more on his cycling interests.

It was then that news reached him of a rift between Laurin and Kraus.

BEGINNINGS – MLADA BOLESLAV

Mlada Boleslav means Young, or in this case the Younger, Boleslav, and refers to the second Bohemian prince to bear the name. A nephew of Good King Wenceslas, Boleslav, who established a castle here in the ninth century, was a force in Christianising the Czech lands. Straddling the River Iser, about 35 miles from Prague, Mlada Boleslav was incorporated as a town in 1528 by Ferdinand I. Having grown from an agricultural settlement, it went on, during the Renaissance, to become the fourth town in Bohemia.

The Thirty Years War and other unpleasantnesses between Prussia and Austria gave the place an almost continual battering for the best part of two centuries, so the peace and quiet ushered in by the reign of Josef II was more than welcome. However, it would be some time before the shell-shocked buildings and residents readjusted to the comparative tranquillity.

Known throughout history for its merchants and craftsmen, Mlada Boleslav remains right at the centre of Central Europe. Its geographical convenience as a theatre of war is just as adaptable to international détente and commerce, so the fact that the meeting of Laurin and Klement took place there was fortuitous on many levels, and continues to be so more than a hundred years later.

For a little while there was a stand-off, as both parties waited to see what the other would do. In reality, neither could afford to jump while he thought the other might set up in opposition to him. Finally it was Laurin who made the first move, asking his lawyer, Zimmermann, to arrange an introductory meeting. Once the two men met, the way forward seemed obvious. Between them they had all the talents necessary to make a commercial engineering undertaking succeed. The two went into partnership and the Laurin and Klement company was born.

Their first application to the town council to build a machine shop was unsuccessful because of inadequate drainage, but a second location was viewed more favourably. Benatska Street was in a not especially salubrious area called Na Hejtmance. In fact, it was locally known as U sedmi zlodeju – the seven thieves – but everyone has to start somewhere.

The unit opened the week before Christmas 1895, and employed two workers and an apprentice, all three of whom, in tandem with the two captains of industry themselves, spent the whole of the long working day at pedal-powered machine tools.

No longer content with a plan to service and repair the cycles that were brought to them, they were at work on producing one of their own. The result was the Slavia velocipede.

Two views of Mlada Boleslav. (Author)

THREE

CYCLES AND MOTORCYCLES

By early 1896 the partners had taken on another six workers and invested in a steam engine to power the tools. The Slavia bicycle, launched to the public in October of that year, was a sophisticated product. Frames were made using steel tubing supplied from Birmingham. Chains, wheels and saddles were imported from specialist suppliers and buyers could specify a deluxe model with the benefit of Continental pneumatic tyres in place of the standard solid rubber items.

Klement's bookshop continued to flourish, under his wife's management, and now had the first franchise for the new velocipedes. Further, he weighed in with an early example of exploitation merchandising in the form of a popular how-to book on the new craze, the catchily titled *Handbook for Cyclists and for those who wish to become them*.

Laurin, in the meantime, had to support his family solely on the proceeds of cycle manufacture. Unsurprisingly the company's collateral was soon used up and they were faced with the commonplace business conundrum of how to finance the making of the product that would ultimately generate their income. If the problem was commonplace, Klement's solution was far from it. When he could no longer borrow from friends, he hit upon the idea of taking the entire Slavia production, except for a few demonstrators, to Mlada Boleslav's leading pawn shop. In return, he was advanced sufficient money to pay wages and continue production. A potential customer would present himself at the Slavia works, where he would be shown a demonstration model. If the sale was concluded, he would pay Laurin and Klement a deposit, and would be sent off to redeem his purchase. Brilliantly original though this idea was, punters were not thrilled about paying over what amounted to a couple of months' wages for something out of a pawn shop. So Klement's next idea was an instalment plan.

Now the customers themselves would pay the production costs through a series of deposits prior to delivery. Again, the theory was fine but in practice a laborious process was set up, which employed local worthies to oversee its ethical operation. On payment of the third instalment the cycle would be delivered to a member of this committee for safe-keeping, pending collection on delivery of the final payment.

An early Laurin & Klement bicycle on show at the Skoda Museum in Mlada Boleslav. (Skoda UK)

Klement went back to the more traditional method of raising finance from the banks, but none of the Czech financial institutions would look at him. Unwavering in his self-belief, he bemoaned their lack of imagination and resolved to bypass them. Bravely he took his prospectus to the extremely serious Landerbank in Germany. Their response was entirely positive. They advanced the money Klement needed on the understanding that a bank employee was permanently installed at Mlada Boleslav to oversee the sensible administration of the funds.

By February 1898 they were doing well enough to build their own brand new factory on the main road to Kosmonosy. This enabled them to expand both production numbers and model range. For the first time a tandem was included in the Slavia catalogue. Later that year, when the factory was fully up and running, Klement set off on a fateful visit to Paris, ostensibly on a fact-finding mission to catch up on any innovations in the cycling world. He found these aplenty, and was also staggered by the degree of motorisation that had taken place in the French capital. Buses, taxis, delivery vans were a world away from the horse economy with which he was familiar. Of more immediate use and inspiration to him, though, was a thing called a 'motorcyclette', produced by Werner Frères. This was a bicycle with a small accessory motor mounted over, and driving, the front wheel – an arrangement that persists in France to this day. Klement bought one at once and brought it back with him to Mlada Boleslav. Wait until Laurin saw this thing. He, like Klement, would know immediately what their next

Early Laurin & Klement
motorcycles *en masse*.
(Skoda UK)

project should be. The firm of Laurin and Klement was going into
motorcycles.

Nowadays new models are tested behind razor wire and 10ft walls. If
they venture on to the public highway they are camouflaged in an effort
to thwart the ever-vigilant spy cameras of the motoring press. In turn-of-
the-century Bohemia things were slightly different. Purpose-designed for
the construction of bicycles, even the new factory had no proving facility.
So when it came to testing their version of the motorcyclette, our heroes
stood or fell in full view of the good citizens of Mlada Boleslav. Inevitably
word had reached them that there was a major new product in
development and they lined the Kosmonosy road ready to roar in
astonishment when Laurin burst upon the scene, tenuously mounted
upon what seemed to be a self-propelled bicycle and accompanied by an
irregular assortment of explosions, splutterings and cries of alarm.

Every possible trial had been undertaken prior to this first public
appearance. Both bicycle and engine had met every criterion. There was
no reason not to believe that Laurin would emerge from the factory gates
and sweep past the rows of admiring onlookers at speeds of up to 35mph.
In the event he was lucky to manage 12mph – and that only by pedalling
for all he was worth.

The engines then available to them operated on the hot-tube ignition
system. There were no sparking plugs such as we have today. A device
similar to a blow-lamp trained its flame on an incandescent platinum

tube. Once the tube was white hot, it would provide the spark needed to fire the internal combustion process. However, no sooner had Laurin left the factory than the wind put the lamp out, the tube cooled and the engine stopped. Rather than the key to effortless motion, this last now became an ungainly dead weight on the handlebars. The onlookers would have had enough to laugh about if Laurin had just pedalled the thing back into the factory. But each dogged rekindling of the lamp, each forward lunge and each ignominious fizzling out redoubled their mirth.

Laurin and Klement never doubted that they would have the last laugh, of course. So, immediately the debacle was over, they set to work to overcome the central problem. Laurin's solution was a windproof metal tube housing for the lamp. This proved successful in mild conditions, but had its limitations in strong winds and rain. Additionally, there were various accidents involving the blow-lamp, including one in which a factory worker was nearly blinded in the middle of a busy street. Electric ignition was tried, but this was not successful either. The batteries required to provide the spark were terribly heavy, had very limited capacity and replacing a discharged unit demanded special tools. So ever more improved versions of the hot tube were persevered with, while Laurin set to work to make his motorised cycle more cohesive and practical. It was clear to him that, rather than a bicycle with an engine grafted on to it, what was needed was a purpose-designed motorcycle – a vehicle with the engine designed in from the start.

His first breakthrough was the decision to take the weight off the handlebars. Perching the engine high above the front wheel had been a fine way to motorise a conventional bike, but it was terribly top-heavy and made steering very difficult. Moving it over on to the frame would both lighten the handlebars and lower the centre of gravity. Chain drive to the rear wheel opened the way to all sorts of possibilities in terms of gearing and increased traction. Gradually, by re-siting the engine and fuel tank in various parts of an evolving frame design until he was happy with them, Laurin arrived at the universal blueprint for the motorbike that remains essentially unaltered to this day. The engine as low as possible in the frame, the fuel tank on the cross bar, forward of the saddle – today, we take this arrangement for granted, but it didn't just happen. It was the result of many man hours of experimentation, and not a few of frustration and personal injury, by one ingenious individual: Vaclav Laurin.

THE MOTORCYCLE COMES OF AGE

Laurin made a business of solving seemingly insoluble engineering problems. He had shaped the future of the motorcycle more or less single-handedly. But he still couldn't lick the ignition problem, which continued to plague motor engineers everywhere. Everywhere, that is, except Stuttgart, where one Robert Bosch had recently patented a low tension

In continuous production for most of the first decade of the twentieth century, the Type L was Laurin & Klement's most popular model. It was offered in 350, 450 and 650cc versions and was regarded as the last word in terms of comfort and equipment levels. (Skoda UK)

This close-up of a Type L saddle suggests their last word was not ours! (Skoda UK)

magneto-electric system. When news of this reached Laurin's ears he knew at once it was the way forward. He already knew an electrical spark was more reliable and capable of being more accurately timed. The use of a magneto would mean that battery life could be extended to months rather than hours.

Laurin and Klement contacted Bosch, but didn't like the price he was charging for what they regarded as untried units. A lengthy correspondence was entered into, during which they tried to persuade him to let them have units on test, or at a reduced price for bulk orders. He could see no purpose in them testing the unit, which was already proving itself with other manufacturers who were prepared to pay. His price was his price, and that's all there was to it. Eventually Klement relented and ordered a unit. Once Laurin had one in his hands, it didn't take him long to replicate it. In fact, he improved upon it, making it much lighter and cheaper to produce.

The first true motorcycle was revealed to press and public at Prague's Bubny Cycle Track on 18 November 1899. The Model A had an output of 1¼ horsepower and the Model B, 1¾. This time the demonstration was a complete success. The motorcycles proved themselves reliable, and comfortably managed speeds of 25mph. Various dignitaries and members

This Type L, preserved in the Skoda Museum, is a late model, from 1907. Drive was still by means of a leather belt and engine lubricating oil was hand-pumped at intervals by the intrepid rider. (Skoda UK)

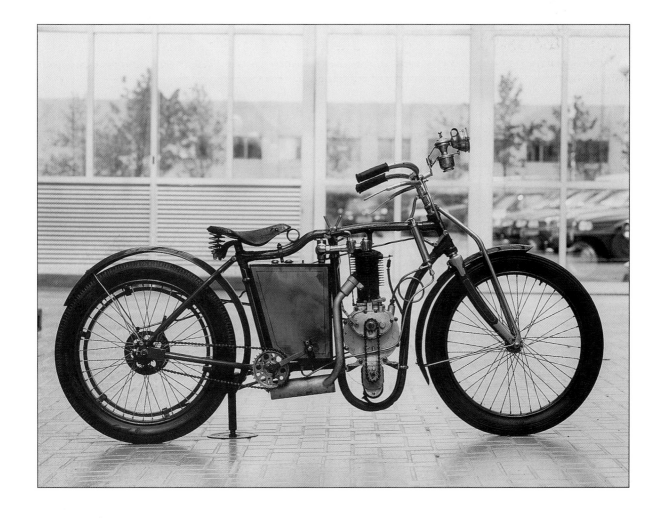

A gratifying number of Laurin & Klement's early motorcycles have survived the mixed fortunes of the nine intervening decades. They make a poignant and impressive display at the Skoda Museum. (Skoda UK)

of the press received summary instruction and took off on the bikes themselves. All of the latter wrote in praise of the machines and their ease of use.

Nobody, however, put their hands in their pockets. No matter how wonderful they thought the new contraptions were, nobody actually wanted to buy one. And not just in Prague or Mlada Boleslav. Klement embarked on a gruelling demonstration tour, criss-crossing Bohemia, but came back with nothing. As he had done in the past, Klement shrugged off his compatriots' lack of imagination and immediately scheduled another tour, this time of Germany. Day after day, at venue after venue, he knocked himself out demonstrating the motorcycle's virtues. He made himself hoarse explaining and reiterating details. But this time it paid off. He returned with thirty-five firm orders, confirming his belief that he must seek success beyond the borders of Bohemia.

Accordingly his next target was the home of his most serious competitors – Britain. He set off for London early in 1900 to look for a British dealer to represent L&K. He thought he had found one, but the individual in question went off on one of the machines and didn't come back. Enlisting the aid of a fellow Czech national with a UK-based business, Laurin lured the man to Tenby, where the bike was restored to its rightful owner. Klement was then introduced to the oldest motor dealer in London – the firm that had first sold the Benz car there. Proprietor Mr Hawetson was so impressed by Klement's demonstration that he ordered 150 machines on the spot.

So Klement returned in glory to Mlada Boleslav, bringing more success than they had dared imagine. But, in combination with the order from Germany, it was also more than they had the manufacturing capacity for. If they could produce the bikes themselves, the newly established department responsible for them had a long way to go before it would be turning ignition units out on that scale. Additionally, nearly two hundred machines consisted of a lot of components and raw materials, for which Laurin and Klement would initially have to foot the bill.

Once again, overcoming a general lack of interest in the project within Bohemia, Klement managed to find an aristocratic backer to underwrite the materials needed and sustain the factory until the returns came in. He also managed to source some Bosch ignition units from Dénes & Friedmann in Vienna. Against all odds, the orders were filled and the machines delivered.

Unfortunately Simms & Co. had exclusive rights to Bosch ignitions in the UK, and the arrival of Laurin & Klement's machines, with their Austrian-sourced units, was brought to their attention. But this time Bosch was inclined to be more reasonable and allowed Hawetson to sell this single consignment, on the understanding that no further breaches of his licence occurred in the future – a surprisingly magnanimous gesture toward a company that had pirated his system to produce their own.

Any nagging doubts about the future, either of the motorcycle, or Laurin & Klement's concentration upon it, now evaporated, and on 3 April 1900 Klement sold the bookshop that had been his liberating force and his mainstay throughout the early life of the firm. He was now fully on board. He and Laurin were in it for the duration and their destiny lay right at the forefront of the golden age of motorcycling.

THE RACE IS ON

Toward the end of 1900, with the factory and its sixty-eight employees running at full capacity on the new machines, Laurin & Klement decided the time had come to exhibit their products on the international stage. Laurin and a number of the other engineers believed the best way to bring them to international attention was to take part in some of the races now beginning to be organised. Klement rejected the idea, claiming there was no value in it, and pointing out that they didn't really have a bike suitable to the purpose. He preferred to go for a nice, static display at a trade show. As ever he won the day, and machines were sent to the International Exhibition at Frankfurt-am-Main, where they won first prize and a gold medal.

Laurin shared Klement's delight at this, but didn't let go of his own dream. For the next round of exhibitions he had something a little different. The Model C had a pillion saddle, and a single-cylinder engine capable of delivering 3 horsepower. Laurin had conceived it with racing in mind. Klement had it exhibited at Prague's International Spring Exhibition, the International Automotive Exhibition in Vienna and the International Exhibition of Automobiles in Hamburg, at all of which it took first prize.

Laurin's mind was already moving on to another challenge. He began to experiment with some prototype four-wheeled vehicles. Though they were simple affairs, they were the first hint of a later move into car production.

Meanwhile, the success of the Model C at the various exhibitions led Klement to have a change of heart. He entered Laurin & Klement in the Paris–Berlin Automobile and Motorcycle Race. He was no daredevil and Laurin could not be spared, even if it had been a dignified thing for a company director to do, so someone had to be chosen as works rider. Narcis Podsednicek had no particular experience or demonstrable aptitude, but he was tall enough for his feet to reach the ground and he had worked his way up to foreman in a matter of months, so Klement volunteered him. The two headed for Paris where, for reasons that are not entirely clear, they shared the same hotel bed. Presumably it was all they could afford. They certainly didn't have the money for spare tyres. As they reported, the following morning, for pre-race registration and warm-ups, this particular shortcoming came home to them.

The roads between Paris and Berlin were not the autoroutes and autobahns of today. They weren't even Nationales. There was no co-ordinated road network at all. Much of the race would take place on rutted cinder tracks, gravel and rock strewn lanes and muddy, root-infested forest paths. Under perfect conditions, the pneumatic tyres of the

day might last 5,000 miles. This kind of punishment could see them off in as many yards. Klement and his driver began to get nervous. They could see the race being lost without the Model C getting a chance to prove itself.

Podsednicek went for a walk that evening and came upon a dressmaker's window, wherein he saw the nightshift working away. A flash of genius came to him that would justify his selection by Klement, even if he fell off at the start of the race, In his best French – shouting and waving his arms about – he explained his idea to the seamstresses and asked whether they thought it would work. Whatever they said heartened him, because he rushed off and brought back the two tyre casings. His idea, to sew a thick textile pad between the casing and the inner-tube, increased potential tyre life by a factor of four, and paralleled the thinking of the Michelin brothers, not a million miles away, in Clermont-Ferrand.

Pod's modified tyres survived the whole race undamaged. He completed the course so far ahead of any of the other competitors that, when he arrived in Berlin at 3 in the morning, the finishing checkpoint was unattended. Unfazed, even at the end of so gruelling a challenge, he decided to go in search of a policeman for official verification of his time of arrival. When the checkpoint finally opened, his action was deemed to

Laurin & Klement began to move toward car production by way of their first motor-tricycle in 1899. This LW tricar dates from around 1905 and is powered by a single-cylinder four-stroke 800cc engine. Oil pumped up by the chauffeur lubricated the engine by drip feed. It was a skilled job pumping enough back up before it all settled in the sump and the engine ran dry. (Skoda UK)

have contravened the race regulations and he was disqualified accordingly. His remonstrations proving useless, he gave up and went to his hotel to warm the bed up for Klement.

Unbeknown to him, the story of his snatched victory reached the spectators and he was soon awoken by a boisterous crowd, come to carry him away and insist upon the proper recognition of his victory. Klement arrived to a cold bed, but the news from the fêted and sated Pod, when his adoring public finally released him, couldn't have been better. Any doubts about Laurin and Klement's raceworthiness evaporated, and he resolved to commit the firm, 100 per cent, to the mushrooming competition circuit.

GLITTERING PRIZES

On their return to Mlada Boleslav Klement put Pod together with Laurin to advise on modifications that had come to light from his racing experience. As a result a design team was formed that added still more innovation and know-how to Laurin's own. The products of this team were not restricted to competition machines, either. Early in 1902 a whole new range of roadgoing bikes were launched, including a so-called ladies' model.

In May of that year Laurin & Klement entered a race to the summit of Mount Exelberg, near Vienna. Klement himself won the 50kg class, in a time of 8 minutes, 17.4 seconds. Pod arrived four seconds later to take second place. Next came the Paris–Vienna – over 2,500 miles of diabolical roads, including the formidable Arlberg pass. Laurin & Klement took third and fourth places and Podsednicek was the only entrant to get over the Arlberg without assistance. In August the first ever motorcycle race was run on Czech soil. Pod won again, with another L&K rider, Zahradka, in second place.

At the beginning of 1903 the factory was expanded to accommodate a new forge, metal works and motor assembly shop. There were now over two hundred employees and the firm's products were becoming ever more sophisticated. They produced their first twin-cylinder bike (Type CC) and commenced sidecar manufacture. The company was awarded a gold medal and a state prize by the Ministry of Trade and secured valuable orders from the military.

In 1904 directors, employees and the world at large were stunned by the news that the Austrian Association of Motorcyclists had chosen the firm to represent Austria in the Gordon Bennett Cup in France. Although naturally honoured and excited, they were also somewhat alarmed at the short notice with which they had to prepare for the high-profile event. Within only two days, they had to be ready to compete on an unfamiliar course, consisting of five separate 30-mile circuits. None the less, Klement could hardly reject the challenge. On arrival, they discovered that their machines didn't conform to race requirements, having neither silencers nor front brakes. They overcame this by buying a bicycle brake and attaching it to the motorbike's handlebars. Then they used rolled metal to fabricate a lookalike silencer. The regulations didn't require that the items operate, merely that they were present.

But another problem revealed itself that was not so easily dealt with. France had moved on to a more advanced form of petrol, designed for their new-fangled fuel-spray carburettors. L&K's engines still used surface-evaporation carbs, which worked perfectly well with lighter, more volatile, Czech petrol. To stand a chance in the competition, Klement had to find a source for this type of fuel. Various oil companies were approached

A Laurin & Klement Type CCR motorcycle takes part in the 1905 International Cup Race. This painting captures the frantic and foolhardy nature of racing in the early part of the last century, when riders launched themselves along dusty, unsurfaced roads, with no reconnaisances or pre-planning – often with no very useful maps. There were no garages, no roadside repairers waiting for them along their epic routes, so they roared onward into uncertainty, loosing their determined grip on the handlebars only periodically to wipe the film of dust and oil from their goggles. (Graham Whyte collection)

without success. Finally Klement contacted the Paris office of Fanta, a firm with interests in Bohemia, and persuaded them to intercede with the one French enterprise that might be able to help them. The intercession was successful, but the fuel stocks were held at some distance from Paris and Klement discovered that French railways didn't permit the carriage of fuel. Showing the same determination and ingenuity that had got him through earlier scrapes, he bought two very large travelling trunks and, concealing the fuel cans inside them, returned to save the day. Only five machines finished the event, three French and both of L&K's. Works rider Toman came in second. His saddle had been lost in a fall, so he placed his cap over the top of the support tube to give himself something slightly softer to sit on.

In 1905 L&K again represented Austria in the Gordon Bennett. Among the other manufacturers taking part were Matchless and Ariel from Britain, Peugeot from France and Puch of Austria. Rider Vondrich, who failed to be placed the previous year, won convincingly, but the trophy was given to the Austrian Motorcyclists' Association. Klement later asked for the loan of it to display at an exhibition and was refused.

The following year, since they were the theoretical victors, the race venue was to be selected by the Austrians. The French were not *terriblement* thrilled by this development, so decided to inaugurate their own grand prix, for which they could make up more acceptable rules. On hearing this, Klement, already a bit shirty about his treatment by the Austrians, was livid and refused to take part. The French then entered a team, after all, but Klement wouldn't be moved. His mind was on new projects; new worlds to conquer. At the height of its success the Laurin & Klement motorcycle racing team had become a thing of the past.

FOUR

THE FIRST CARS

TAKING STOCK

On 1 January 1907 Laurin and Klement set about transforming the firm into a joint-stock company. Where, until then, it had been a private concern, with all risks and profits due to the two titular heads, it would now become an entity unto itself. It would have shareholders and directors, and limited liability. Laurin and Klement would be somewhat distanced from their original proprietorial roles in favour of management and a regular salary. In addition, as part of its constitution, 10 per cent of any profits would be divided between Klement and Laurin, on a sixty-forty ratio. Klement was named General Manager and Laurin Technical Manager. There were now more than six hundred workers employed at Mlada Boleslav, and satellite offices of the company existed in Prague, Vienna and Budapest.

The previous year the company had exhibited its first car, the Type A Voiturette, at various automotive shows. Like the cycles and motorcycles before it, it gained instant public and professional approbation, winning L&K its first gold medal for automobiles from the German Autoklub.

The Laurin & Klement factory. (Skoda UK)

Now production of four-wheeled vehicles was stepping up. In July 1907 public transport came to Moscow with the arrival of three Laurin & Klement light omnibuses. The company's engine plant was also coming into its own. Its Type F 2.5-litre side-valve unit incorporated sparking plugs and HT (High Tension) ignition. A monstrous 5-litre affair, designated FF, was produced by joining two Fs together!

The move to four wheels was also allowing L&K to play a part in the commerce of the country in a way never before possible. Their Type E commercials were shifting food, livestock, coal and machinery. The 6-litre Type H 4-tonner would move anything they couldn't manage. No time was wasted bringing these new products to the world. Vehicles and marketing staff were involved in a continual tour of exhibitions and promotional events, in Paris, Leipzig, Berlin and St Petersburg.

Although the motorcycling team had been disbanded, the competition element hadn't been forgotten either. Proven champion motor racing driver Otto Hieronimus was taken on as a full-time employee as the works competition driver – on the second highest salary, after Klement's.

Two views of the engine construction shop.
(Skoda UK)

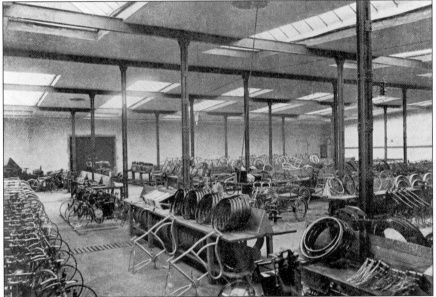

Three early factory
photographs: bicycle,
motorbike and car production
shared the same premises.
(Skoda UK)

In January 1908 company foreman Tuta set off to Prague as its first bus driver, in a HOP (Heavy Omnibus Prague) bus, specially designed for the city, to take part in trials that would lead, three months later, to the introduction of a regular service.

Montenegro, now part of Yugoslavia, has some of the most spectacular and challenging roads to be found anywhere. In order to find vehicles capable of dealing with the sheer switchback ascents (and descents) from the Bay of Kotor to the capital, Cetinje, the Montenegrins organised a design competition, which L&K won, with some highly innovative forward control commercials.

Under Hieronimus, the competition department started to bear fruit. L&K cars took six firsts, five seconds and a third in the Bosnia section of the Ivanpass event. Sasha Kolowrat's 2-litre Laurin & Klement beat a 3-litre car to first place in the race to Ries. Hieronimus won his class and came in fifth overall in the St Petersburg–Moscow. Rezler won the Vienna–Klagenfurt–Vienna and L&K cars won every class at Semmering.

Away from the racetracks, more pedestrian developments were occurring. A licence to build Brons diesel stationary engines for electricity generation demanded more manufacturing space. Klement and Hieronimus had loftier ideas. In 1910 the latter managed to safely take off, fly about and land in an aircraft powered by an engine of his own design. Klement brought the board of directors along to see him do it again, but couldn't persuade them to go into aeroplane production.

In September of that year motorcycle production at Mlada Boleslav came to an end. Almost 4,000 examples had been produced altogether. In those days, pre-mass production, that was a serious number. The Slavia name was also discontinued.

In a Europe whose main industry was agriculture, much of the progress in engineering was driven by the needs of farmers. This six-bladed P4 motor-plough caused a sensation in the countryside and the horses were right to be very afraid. (Skoda UK)

ON A ROLL

Mass production had arrived in America. A farmer called Henry Ford was knocking out automobiles fast enough to far exceed domestic demand, and it was beginning to look as if he could end up filling Europe with them too. Klement saw that he would need to get in first if he wanted a piece of any personal transport revolution that might be coming along. In April 1911 the Type S was launched, with a four-cylinder, 1771cc engine delivering 14hp. The unusual design featured a forward flywheel, multi-plate clutch and integrated engine and gearbox, using a shared oil supply.

But before any such revolution could get much of a hold there would need to be something more like a road for the new motorists to travel on. So Klement joined with the Prague Engineering Company to produce road rollers.

Hieronimus continued to be unstoppable. He won the almost unbelievably arduous September Rally in Russia, along with Kolowrat, Dorring and Donier, before going straight on to win the Caucasus Cup. L&K cars also took third and fifth places.

The answer to future prosperity also lay in the soil, and Klement entered into another co-manufacturing agreement to produce mammoth 50hp motor ploughs. Fifty-one of these were built between 1912 and 1914.

Also in 1912 Laurin & Klement acquired the rights to the superbly smooth and quiet Knight engines from America, thanks to the purchase of a firm called RAF (Reichenberger Automobilfabriek). Only Minerva in Belgium, Mercedes in Germany and Panhard of France had the rights to these engines. Klement wanted to know how Minerva achieved its superior results with these engines, so he sent an L&K engineer called Plachy to Belgium to spy on them. He was discovered and sent back to Mlada Boleslav in 1913, but Klement employed him as his personal driver with a good salary and an additional clothing allowance as a reward for his undercover work.

1913 saw the end of chain drive, even on heavy commercials, and the gradual introduction of electric, rather than acetylene, lights. Roadbuilding was continuing apace, and L&K delivered a further twenty-five road rollers.

The following year, thanks to a shooting incident in Belgrade, the bottom fell out of people's cars and motor racing. Even Plachy's clothing allowance lost some of its magic. The world of daredevils, of infinite possibility, of innovation and diversification was no more. Its peoples were embroiled in a war to end all wars that was nothing of the kind. The First World War was upon them: a new kind of war that included everyone.

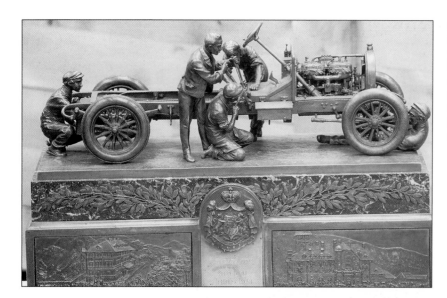

Prince Erich Thurn-Taxis was a champion of industry who put up a prize of ten thousand crowns and this trophy for the best car factory. Laurin & Klement entered the various trials devised by the Austrian Automobile Club, including endurance test and hill-climbs, winning the award hands down in 1911. (Skoda UK)

Laurin & Klement's first real car was the Type A Voiturette. Produced between 1905 and 1907, it was powered by a V-twin water-cooled 1e-litre engine, driving the rear wheels. Most examples were shaft driven, though some – especially commercial variants – used chain drive. In either case a differential was employed, either as part of the rear axle or, in chain-driven models, at the back of the gearbox. Capable of speeds of up to 25mph, it relied on a transmission brake to bring it to a standstill. (Skoda UK)

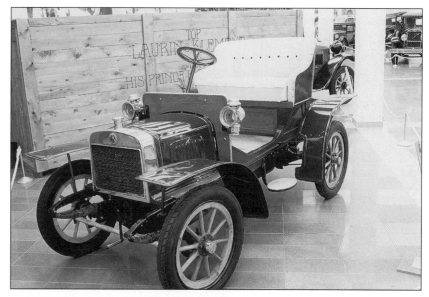

Laurin and Klement were well aware of the need for an easily identifiable trademark. Their motor logo incorporated not only the firm's name fashionably spelled out in art deco characters, but a laurel wreath to symbolise their numerous sporting successes. (Skoda UK)

The Type B Voiturette of 1907 benefited from a 1.4 litre version of the V-twin that could power it along at closer to 30mph and made it even more of a challenge to stop. (Skoda UK)

This variant was one (horse) removed from a hansom cab, which at least afforded the passenger some protection from the Bohemian winter. (Skoda UK)

By the time the Type C came along, things were getting a bit more sophisticated. Different chassis lengths allowed for the possibility of a multitude of bodywork options, from delivery vans to phaetons, such as this 1907 example, containing Vaclav Laurin and family. Types B and C were produced in tandem, the latter distinguished by its 2-litre engine and a top speed that smashed through the 30mph barrier. (Skoda UK)

This 1908 Type F is also a pretty substantial contraption. Versions of it (FF) were available with straight-eight engines of up to 5-litre capacity, though this one is a relatively modest 2.5-litre four. (Skoda UK)

The G Series appeared in 1909, by which time Laurin & Klement's reputation had spread well beyond the boundaries even of the Austro-Hungarian Empire. Here's proof that women had a handle on the business of motoring way back then in this wonderful picture of a G2 Sports, taken in Japan. (Skoda UK)

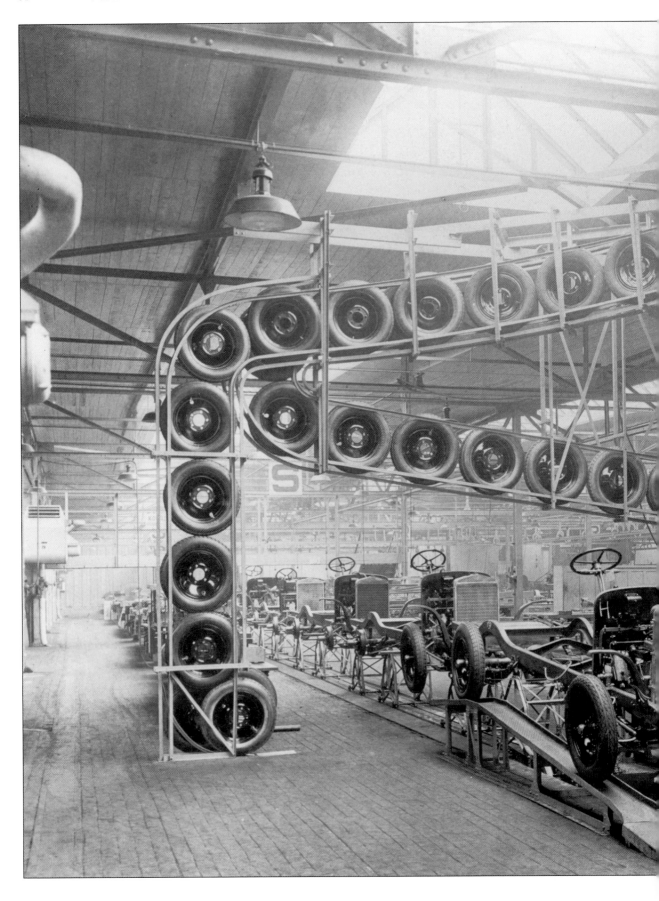

Where there's a wheel. Modern mass-production techniques weren't developed all at once. This clever construction speeded up the assembly process by delivering wheels to both sides of the line, but getting them aloft for gravity to do its work would have been fairly labour-intensive before the advent of pallets and the fork-lift. (Skoda UK)

Laurin & Klement's victorious entrant in the Zbraslav–Jiloviste race of 1908. (Graham Whyte collection)

A 2-litre Type F Laurin & Klement at the completion of the Petrograd to Moscow race in the same year. (Graham Whyte collection)

Not a minaret to lose. This depicts a Type FC car in the 2,000 kilometre Bosnian endurance trial in 1908. (Graham Whyte collection)

Note here how romantic is the scenery around Mlada Boleslav (above) by comparison with the bleak industrial landscape of Brooklands (right). (Graham Whyte collection)

And here's a similar car in the Alps, the following year. (Graham Whyte collection)

You can't park there, guv. Head of the London office of Laurin & Klement, Frantisek Toman, thinks he owns the road in his 1911 Type S. (Skoda UK)

AN ILL WIND

The outbreak of war didn't augur awfully well for Laurin & Klement at the start. But, like other engineering enterprises elsewhere in the world, they soon found themselves carried along by the inevitable demand for their expertise. Initially car production was suspended at Mlada Boleslav and the company ordered to concentrate on the production of shells. This provided unprecedented levels of employment for men who at first thought the war would put them out of a job. Klement determined to make the most of the opportunities and his genius for turning problems to advantages was never better demonstrated than during this time of uncertainty and limited resources. The need for military vehicles was recognised soon enough by the politicos and military commanders, so production soon resumed – in new buildings constructed by Klement alongside those now dedicated to the production of ordnance.

Looking very advanced for its time, this articulated Type 500 military transport employed the Martin semi-trailer system. Powered by an engine of four huge cylinders, displacing a total of 4713cc, it peaked at 38bhp and relied for its stopping power on the ubiquitous transmission brake. (Skoda UK)

Heavy restrictions had been placed upon the movement of food and supplies, so it was difficult for those working at the L&K factory to obtain food for sick friends and relatives, even if they had money, or other items to barter. But all the new vehicles ordered by the military needed running in prior to delivery. So Klement planned a route for them that would take in farms, abattoirs, grain stores and other places of supply. There is even

a story told of a whole pig being delivered to the factory during the test run of a new hearse, sealed in a genuine coffin.

Probably justified in his conviction that he was able to do any one of their jobs better, Klement had been vocal in his criticism of the Austrian government, both before and during the war. With loyalties strained by a conflict or equally unlovable masters, this led to unwelcome official attention. At one point the government threatened to take over the company, though this was mercifully prevented by one of Klement's better connections. However, a certain amount of suspicion remained and the factory was raided on at least one occasion by the State Police. Nothing untoward was found, but Klement was accused of being a Russian sympathiser – a proposition he greeted with laughter and derision. It is perhaps to the authorities' credit that, rather than take offence at this, they went away and left him alone.

Klement treated their meddling with complete unconcern. His vision was at work on a larger project. Gradually, over the course of the war, he worked to make Mlada Boleslav ever more self sufficient. Workshops within the factory were set up to make shoes for the workers. A butchery, a smokery and an inn were bought by the company to serve the workforce. Even the purchase and repairing of clothes could be carried out within the factory walls. At the same time the actual machinery of production was continually upgraded. Klement wanted to house the entire manufacturing process, from raw material to showroom product, under the same roof.

Gradually Mlada Boleslav turned into a model operation. Everything the workers needed to live and everything the manufacturing process required to go forward was in place by the middle of the war. There

One kind of vehicle for which there was no falling off in demand during the war was ambulances. While the rest of the factory concentrated on the production of shells and grenades, the automotive production lines were kept busy producing vehicles that would see service at the front. (Skoda UK)

The four-seater Type O.
(Skoda UK)

were shops, restaurants and sporting facilities, foundries, timber yards and precision gear shops. Only the reliance on coal from distant fields left L&K vulnerable to external influences. Klement had an answer for that, too. Two kilometres from the factory an old mill on the Jizera River was converted to supply exclusive hydroelectric power to the works, removing the dependency on steam power and greatly reducing costs.

At Pilsen, Skoda, too, could be said to be having a good war. The demand for armaments from the empire had done for Skoda what similar British, French and German contracts had done for Vickers, Schneider and Krupps respectively. By the end of the war, on paper, the Skoda company's future was assured.

The 2.5-litre Type O Phaeton came in two lengths to accommodate either four or six passengers. It could also be had as a limousine, landaulette or various two-, three- and four-seater sports cars. Lubrication had long since graduated to a proper circulation pump and filter, and early evaporation carburettors had given way to rather more sophisticated items from Zenith. (Skoda UK)

Motors tended toward the substantial in those days. When something like this turned up, you knew it had arrived. By this time engines were becoming more efficient and capacities reduced accordingly. The Sd was powered by a 1.8-litre four, delivering a whole 20bhp. (Skoda UK)

Production of the Type S, including Phaetons such as these examples preserved in the Skoda Museum, continued through the first half of the war. The 1771cc engine needed to be pretty forgiving, with a body of this size and only a three-speed box. (Skoda UK)

Curtains in the back, and not even any glass in the front – this chauffeur knew his place. But the fine MK Limousine was built for President Masaryk's wife, Charlotte, as peace returned, in 1919. (Skoda UK)

The MK range was a particularly classy one. As well as the posh limo for Madame M., there was this business-like Phaeton, with its neatly stowed folding roof. Their 3.3-litre four-cylinder engines used Knight sleeve-valves and delivered 40bhp, which could propel them along at 35mph. The driver still had only a transmission footbrake and a handbrake acting on the rear drums to call upon when planning a stop. (Skoda UK)

Until the end of the First World War wooden wheels predominated on Laurin & Klement cars, as on most others. Wire wheels could be had as an option, but were both cheaper and flimsier than the former on the broken roads of that period. In 1918 Michelin pressed steel wheels became available. They were less prone to damage than either of the other options and proved to be the forerunner of modern car wheels. Instantly identifiable from their solid profile, they are seen here on a 8h Phaeton. (Skoda UK)

Type Sg was powered by an 1847cc engine, which drove the rear wheels via a 'torque-tube'. Unlike the regular S models, this had four forward speeds and could hit 40mph on a run. (Skoda UK)

The 100 (also known as the Type A) appeared in 1922 with a 1791cc side-valve engine whose casing also accommodated the four-speed gearbox. The car's 25 bhp enabled it to shatter the 50mph barrier. (Skoda UK)

AFTERMATH

Self-determination had been a dream of the Czech and Slovak people for generations. Now that the outcome of the First World War had spelled doom to the Hapsburg dynasty, they dared to dream it again. On greens and squares all over the country, ragged nationalists foregathered to demand their rights from uninterested riot police and militia. Everyone was so tired after four years of conflict, their old certainties scattering like the dust of yesterday's invincible empire, that there was little fervour in the nationalism and the forces of order barely went through the motions of repression. Mlada Boleslav's local uprising passed off without incident, and within two months the Republic of Czechoslovakia was born.

Wartime restrictions on fuel and the use of private transport were not brought to an end by this monumental development, however. If the war proper had run its course, minor skirmishes and insurgencies continued for many months. With the old order overthrown, there were new precedences to settle, new boundary lines to be drawn, and while this continued the new government was too preoccupied to consider reconstruction of the motor industry. Worse, from Laurin and Klement's point of view, was the fact that the majority of vehicles supplied for wartime use had been commandeered without payment. In the prevailing circumstances there was no immediate prospect of any kind of reparation.

In the event, three long years would pass before contingency ordinances on private motoring were finally rescinded and, even then, there was little encouragement for the staff or management at L&K. With the reconstruction of agriculture, clothing industries and essential

Newly elected president Tomas Masaryk poses with Laurin and Klement and other movers and shakers at Mlada Boleslav as normal service was resumed after the First World War. (Skoda UK)

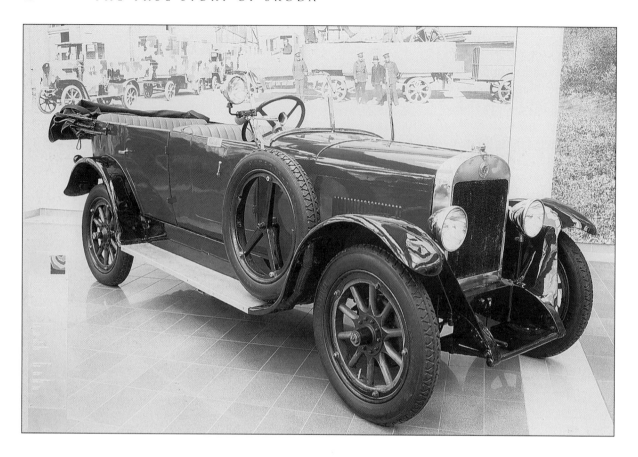

The popularity of the 100 continued well into the 1920s. Versatile and reliable, it did a lot to establish L&K cars as the backbone of daily life between the wars. (Skoda UK)

services uppermost in their thoughts, the new government still had little time for the future of the motor car. If its ministers thought about it at all, it was merely as a useful contributor to treasury coffers. Nowadays we have come to expect nothing more. The people at L&K had dared to hope for better things from their long-awaited national representatives and were doubly wounded by the swingeing fuel and luxury taxes that militated against their commercial survival. And, as if that wasn't enough, they were further attacked in an already difficult enough market-place by the presence of cut-price foreign vehicles, a consequence of Czechoslovakia's minimal import tariffs.

Klement campaigned tirelessly, on his own behalf and that of the motor industry as a whole, for the raising of tariffs and the reduction of inimical taxation. Unlike most of the other combines he represented, L&K, having lost its market for shells and weaponry, was now wholly dependent upon vehicle production for its survival. Fortunately, though the private car market had been blighted by legislation, other L&K products were doing rather better. The firm's mammoth Excelsior motor-ploughs were perfectly suited to the epic and soul-destroying task of turning the French landscape, ravaged by the war, into productive agricultural land. In combination with the relaxation of restrictions and the raising of duties, increasing Europe-wide exports of agricultural machinery enabled the company to enter the 1920s with a degree of optimism.

Car production resumed, and the company set about making their models better than ever, to compete with the quality and comfort of the imported

makes that had found favour during the period of low tariffs. Additionally, the government wanted to capitalise on the growth in commercial aviation, so offered incentives to car manufacturers to develop aero-engines. Klement's energies continued to keep the enterprise going. L&K were more than able to produce world-class cars and to meet any other engineering demands. If they had a problem, it was in the sales department. The cars they were making were actually too good for the domestic market – and, accordingly, too expensive. Klement had set out to deliver Czechoslovakia's answer to the people's car, but had wound up producing something more refined and rarefied, leaving competitors, such as Tatra and Praga, to take the major share of the market. The motor parc in twenties Czechoslovakia seems minuscule by today's international sales standards, with best-selling models ranked in the high fifties but, though they were ticking over with agricultural and aeronautical manufacture, it was pivotal to L&K's future survival.

Klement was in no doubt about the seriousness of the issue, or he wouldn't have taken an action that would change the whole course of events. A disastrous fire at Mlada Boleslav in the summer of 1924 could have brought about the demise of the company, but it was not this that inspired Klement to look for new solutions. He needed the financial muscle to develop an entirely new home-grown car with which to mobilise the people of a country lagging behind the rest of the western world in private motor transport. There's no doubt he would have preferred to pull it off without outside assistance but, in the final analysis, the project was bigger than his own pride.

In the majority of cases, comfortably orf visitors to Prague in the roaring twenties would have come by train. Waiting for them at the station would have been something akin to this Laurin & Klement Type 500 Hotel Bus, seen outside the Grand Hotel in 1924. Featuring Michelin disc wheels, torque transmission tube and very generous ground clearance, the 500 bus provided appropriate space and comfort for guests. A railed roof was designed to accommodate the majority of cases. (Skoda UK)

Numerous models grew out of the success of the 100, this 120 Phaeton, for example. Mechanically and structurally similar, it offered much more power (30bhp) from its 1944cc engine. Capable of reaching 60mph in a favourable wind, this 1925 example still relied on a transmission brake to rein it in. From 1927 four-wheel drums appeared on the options list. If you specified this arrangement, you wound up with a handbrake that worked on the drive shaft, rather than the standard rear drums. (Peter Grenfell)

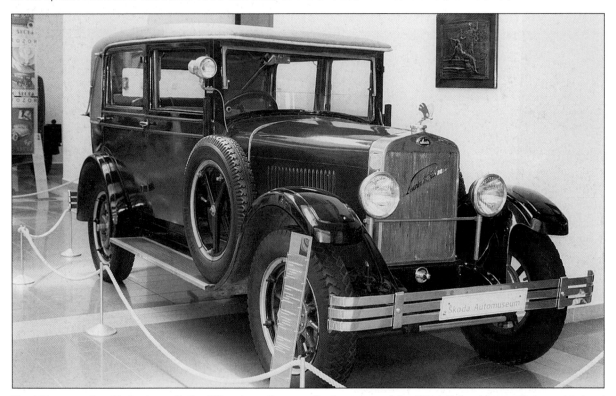

The 110 was produced in tandem with the 120 and was the more direct successor of the 100, initially relying on the same tried and tested 1791cc water-cooled four. In 1926 it gained the 120's 1944cc unit, improving both pulling power and performance. This 110/X1 dates from the final year of production, 1929. It is branded Laurin & Klement – Skoda and features bodywork by British coachbuilders Weymann. World renowned before manufacturers moved to in-house bodybuilding, their name lives on in buses and underground trains bearing the 'MCW' plate – Metro-Cammell (from the Metropolitan Cammell Carriage and Wagon Company) Weymann. (Peter Grenfell)

A close-up of the 1920s Skoda prow: 'flying' mascot on the radiator cap, Skoda badge, and flowing Laurin & Klement 'signature'. (Peter Grenfell)

The 110 was also offered with a natty interchangeable rear end, which turned it from workaday utility to something suitable for promenading Madame and the little ones at weekends. (Peter Grenfell)

A touring body on the same chassis. (Peter Grenfell)

The 1195cc Skoda Type 422 kicked off the 1930s in real style. Despite a return to three-speed gears (until 1934), the car offered new levels of sophistication to the average motorist, both in terms of the more modern integrated look of the bodywork and in the mechanical department. Four-wheel drum brakes and the abandonment of magneto ignition in favour of a dynamo and distributor, a single dry plate clutch, 45mph top speed and around 30 miles to the gallon was as good as it got back then. (Peter Grenfell)

The longer wheelbase 430 shared most of the 422's elements, but was powered by a 1661cc engine. Like the smaller car, the 430 now came as standard with solid disc wheels and was available in various forms – straight chassis, two- and four-door saloons, roadsters, coupés and phaetons. (Peter Grenfell)

A still more powerful model, 430D, had a displacement of 1802cc. Models in the 430 range had particularly smooth and refined engines, thanks to a doubling of the number of crankshaft main bearings to six, by comparison with the then more usual three, as on the 422. The 430 had a top speed of 50mph and turned in about 27mpg. (Peter Grenfell)

FIVE

EMPIRE-BUILDING

COMINGS AND GOINGS

By this time Skoda was a vast manufacturing empire, ranking among the biggest in Europe. But, for all its commercial prominence and far-reaching diversification, its incursions into the motoring world had been hesitant and aimless. Furthermore, having no original product, its involvement had relied entirely upon imports, so the hike in tariffs had effectively put an end to it.

If Klement was reticent about bringing his proposal to Pilsen, no such sentiment troubled the waiting Skoda board. An original model aimed at the mass market was just what they were lacking. They had the production capacity, the distribution, the connections – both locally and internationally – and they had the investment capital. It was all ready to mobilise as soon as they found the right product. In that place and time there could be no better pedigree than by Laurin & Klement out of Skoda. And there could be no better bet for Skoda shareholders.

The two companies officially merged on 1 January 1926, by which time Laurin & Klement's distribution network, materials – and even the Mlada Boleslav workforce – had all been vested in the new parent Skoda company. Although the L&K name survived for the moment and the Mlada Boleslav plant continued as its production base, administrative changes inevitably followed on the heels of the merger. Ordering and distribution functions were centralised in Prague, and Skoda appointed one of its own company men as factory manager.

Laurin and Klement were given courtesy titles, though the former withdrew from active participation in the business from the moment of the Skoda tie-up. Klement remained to oversee the changes he had set in train. Before the old year was out, however, events gathered their own momentum, and he was swept aside by the headlong rush he had himself initiated. Just as it was too late for any regrets, it is pointless now to speculate on the motives and self-doubts that must have assailed him in that fateful year, while his and Laurin's life's work was being picked over and eaten up by out-of-town corporate types. The decision that sidelined him – that divested him of power in the world he had created – had been his own. He had sacrificed his own interests for the better prosecution of

his dream. And there can be little doubt that his actions then were crucial to the fact that his heritage lives on with us today, entering into its second century.

UNDER NEW MANAGEMENT

On paper, the vehicles produced following the merger were to be known as Laurin & Klement – Skodas. In reality, of course, the appellation was far too cumbersome to persist for long, and within a couple of years the Skoda name stood alone in most people's minds.

The 1920s saw a meteoric rise in motor transport in Czechoslovakia, so it is sadly ironic that the forgotten names were those of the individuals whose energy and invention had fuelled it. But now Skoda held the reins. Their management would be different from the family approach of Laurin & Klement. The multitude of pioneers from Mlada Boleslav, each of whom had contributed personally to automotive development, began to disperse; to fade away. They had played their part and diligence, rather than initiative and individual input, was what was required by the new owners.

These were new times. There were new challenges. Klement's dream of the proliferation of private transport was on the verge of becoming a reality. And, as he had had the vision to realise, the big Skoda

All present and correct. The thing to be seen in, as the twenties gave way to the thirties, was something like this Type 645 Limousine Landaulette, which enabled you both to see and – weather permitting – be seen. Power came from a 2.5-litre straight-six with no fewer than eight main bearings. The chauffeur had only three gears to play with, but it would do 60mph; eventually. Nearly eight hundred of these upmarket motors were built between 1929 and 1934. (Skoda UK)

In the days when all cars were handbuilt, using traditional craft methods, building limousines was a sounder proposition than it is today. It helped to have more counts and princes per square hectare than was usual even then, but it's curious to think that there were enough people in that bracket choosing Skoda before a ready variety of other options to buy eight hundred Type 645s and nearly a thousand of these Type 4Rs in only six years. The 4R used a four-cylinder engine of 1944cc. A further three hundred customers stumped up for the longer wheelbase, six-cylinder, 3-litre Type 6R – shown here. (Skoda UK)

corporation's approach was the one that would achieve it. Founder Emil Skoda had already been dead for twenty-five years. His name and reputation had passed into legend before a single car bearing his badge came off the production line.

Nowadays the name of Skoda is known throughout the world, almost exclusively for the cars that mobilised a nation. At this point in a chequered history of wars, ideologies, self-rule and occupation, Skoda's future is looking better than ever. Its past, following Laurin and Klement's departure, is the story of hundreds of less easily identifiable, usually uncredited, individuals. The true story of Skoda is that of a unique motoring heritage – a trail blazed by fearless pioneers and consolidated by hard-headed engineers. In the Skoda of today the same original qualities exist. The ever more discriminating demands of popular private transport go hand in hand with the eternal challenges of motorsport.

Now that Skoda, in turn, has fused with the worldwide Volkswagen Group, the names and the traditions of Laurin and Klement are to the fore again. Come war, come political change, come merger, come recession, come good jokes or bad, the spirit of the original believers has held firm. It comes down to us as one of the finest examples of the creative vision and energy that has characterised the history of the motor industry.

YESTERDAY'S MEN

Under the new régime, no more money was to be 'wasted' on racing and rallying. Skoda's unromantic accountants wanted to see any profits reinvested in future product development. The austerity principle was vindicated by the general financial climate around the world and the earth-shattering repercussions of the Wall Street Crash of 1929. Since the war even its erstwhile enemies had held America up as the model of industrial and economic might. New York's stock market crash shook the foundations of institutions and industrial conglomerates way beyond the United States.

Removed from events, Laurin became aimless and despondent. Already in ill health, he faded rapidly following the merger. Within three years he was admitted to a Prague sanatorium, suffering from intestinal cancer. His wife, Emilie, couldn't contemplate life without him. Grief stricken by his decline, she died on the last day of November 1930. Laurin followed her on 3 December.

Klement had always had a life away from the factory, a fact that helps to explain his willingness to step aside when he deemed it beneficial to the future of the Czech motor industry. In his retirement he continued to be a force to be reckoned with. Recognising the need to record and codify the accomplishments of the new technology, he devoted himself to the production of a history of the automobile, the researching of which involved undertaking a gruelling tour of the United States. Co-written with Czech journalist Vilém Heinz, the book was published in 1931. It had been a labour for Klement, and his old energy was running out at

Another in a long line of faithful family servants, the Skoda Type 633 was manufactured between 1931 and 1934. This one, preserved at the Skoda Museum, dates from 1933. Its engine is a four-cylinder, side-valve unit of 1792cc, delivering 33bhp at a relaxed 3,000rpm. It would do 60mph, but you'd be lucky to get much more than 25mpg out of it. (Peter Grenfell)

last. He suffered a series of strokes, and when his beloved Antonie died in 1935 his will to live went with her.

He had led an extremely full and active life and achieved greatness in his own time. His loss to the motoring world was great, but his legacy, like that of the other pioneering geniuses of the early twentieth century, was the greater.

HARD TIMES

There comes a point in the expansion of any business where it outgrows the constraints of a family concern; a time when the sentiment of those that created and nurtured it becomes not merely dispensable, but an actual obstacle to future progress. The Skoda corporation was devoid of such sentimentality, seeing the new automobile enterprise not as a personal crusade, but as another division to be made profitable.

The timing of Klement's decision to move over couldn't have been better. Only hard-nosed economics would offer a chance of survival through the global upheavals of the twenties and thirties. Certainly, Skoda had been keen to acquire the Mlada Boleslav operation, but it would have to take its place alongside existing successful activities, such as the production under licence of Sentinel steam lorries and Hispano-Suiza luxury cars. When the depression caused the latter's sales to plummet, even greater pressure was put on Laurin and Klement's old team.

In spite of demands for economies and austerity, innovation hadn't been stifled entirely. At only 1792cc, the L&K Skoda 633 of 1931 was the smallest capacity six-cylinder car ever produced. But still there was no sign of the kind of explosion in private motoring that was happening elsewhere. All of Czechoslovakia's major motor manufacturers were struggling. The staff at Mlada Boleslav had been reduced by two-thirds and annual production fell below the two thousand mark. Designers, engineers and factory workers all knew how tenuous their future was if they failed to deliver the goods. With results like these, Skoda would have been justified in closing them down at any time. But someone must have stayed the accountants' hands just long enough for the old firm to prove itself one last time.

POPULAR MOVE

Like other people's cars, such as Dr Porsche's Volkswagen, Pierre Boulanger's Citroën 2CV and Dante Giacosa's Fiat Topolino, Skoda's entry, when it came, was no mere adaptation of an existing model range. Radical design revisions were involved in its development and the car was designed from the ground up.

Most cars then available were constructed on a traditional 'ladder' chassis – so called because it consisted of a number of cross-members,

The story goes that Skoda cars got the name, Tudor, from the English 'two-door', and it's been repeated so often I suppose we must believe it. Bohemians have a sense of humour all their own, which even extends to applying the name to later four-door models. This, anyway, is a two-door Tudor – the Type 420 Standard of 1933. This was a real economy car, capable of doing more than 40mpg. Its 995cc engine delivered 20bhp. Note the rare deviation, during the thirties, from front-opening 'suicide' doors. (Skoda UK)

The most coherently styled little car Skoda had yet produced, the 420 Popular would turn out to be just that, and remain so with motoring aficionados to this day. Using the same engine as the 420 Standard, it benefited from a factory-built body, based on the new backbone chassis. (Skoda UK)

each of which was connected to two main longitudinal girders, or 'longerons'. From a static point of view, this arrangement supplied the ideal frame for the purpose of carrying engine and mechanical components, while forming a perfect base for body construction by outside coachbuilders, in the usual practice of the time. Dynamically speaking, the ladder chassis was less successful. Its heavy metal structure was a burden to performance and handling, contributing much more weight than was desirable. It also lacked torsional rigidity, leading to rattles, structural deformations and all kinds of dynamic difficulties that still plague architects of the motor car to this day. Additionally, the cast and welded structure was prone to fracture when subjected to sudden impacts or shocks – an everyday hazard on the broken and largely unsurfaced causeways faced by the majority of pre-war motorists.

The new Skoda 420 would break away from tradition completely. Its factory-produced standard body would be mounted on a clever new chassis based around a rigid 'backbone', which ran along the middle of the car and divided into V-sections at either end, to support the engine and axles.

Front axles at this time almost universally comprised a single beam mounted on longtitudinal leaf springs. Independent suspension was a rarity, even on sports models. Rear axles, likewise, consisted of a rigid

The top two of the Popular's three forward gears received synchromesh, suspension went all independent and the old worm and nut steering gave way to lighter, more precise rack and pinion. The favoured system by most manufacturers today, this was a rarity in the mid-thirties, and would remain so for another three decades, despite its almost simultaneous adoption by Citroën on its 7A (Traction Avant), also in 1934. (Skoda UK)

This 1936 Popular shows how well original factory-built bodywork could incorporate practical elements into the design, such as the spare wheel, which had often been treated as an afterthought by specialist coachbuilders. As neat as it looks, of course, a 16-inch wheel and tyre adds a bit to the weight of the bootlid. (Skoda UK)

unit, containing differential and half-shafts, and suspended on longtitudinal leaves. All of the other people's cars above benefited from all-independent suspension. Britain's contender, Alec Issigonis's Morris Minor, would arrive in 1948 with a conventional rigid rear axle, but independent front suspension by longtitudinal torsion bars. Uniquely, Skoda's version retained the rigid front axle – though now suspended by quarter-elliptical leaf springs – and gained an independent rear end, employing Hans Ledwinka's ingeniously simple swing axles. This system, which was also adopted by Porsche for the VW, used no complex geometry to keep the driven wheels vertical to the road surface. Both swing arms pivoted from the central differential housing, so vertical movements at the wheel end described an arc. This accounts for the splayed appearance of these cars when laden.

As technologically interesting as the new car was, and as timely as its appearance might have appeared, it was not, in any sense, immediately popular. Such expansion as was building in the Czech market was being better exploited by Skoda's competitors who, rather than expending thousands on elegant automotive developments, were knocking out microscopic bog-standard cyclecars at equally pocket-sized prices.

The change came when the young engineer Josef Zubaty was assigned to do the pre-war equivalent of a remix or a makeover. Remarkably experienced for one of his years, Zubaty was better known to the public as a motoring journalist. But the motor industry itself was not all that old

The catalogue prototype for the Popular Sport has most of the elements that would make it into the production car: 1385cc side-valve engine, driving the rear wheels via a torque tube in the middle of the lightweight skeleton backbone chassis, the last word in sporty styling and a top speed of around 70mph. Its hydraulic brakes and independent suspension fitted it for rapid progress, though a return to worm and nut steering gear seems surprising for a car destined for competition. (Skoda UK)

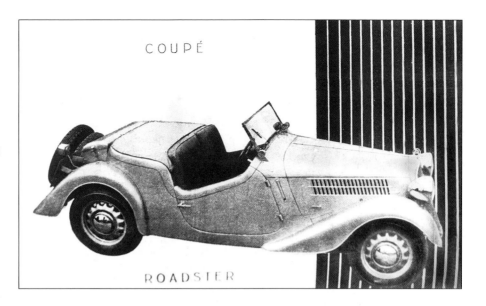

COUPÉ

ROADSTER

COUPÉ

This so-called 'Monte Carlo' coupé derivative of the Popular Sport lost a bit of its prototype streamlining (left) before it entered series production (below). This gave it more of a corporate identity with other Skoda models, and the move from rounded to inclined grille doesn't seem to have effected its wind-resistance. It finished third in its class in the 1937 Monte Carlo Rally. (Skoda UK)

Possibly the world's most photogenic Skoda, this jolly red Type 421 Rapid Cabriolet is one of the stars of the museum in Mlada Boleslav. Dating from 1937, it is small and beautifully formed. Among its unusual features is a central pump that provides automatic chassis lubrication. (Peter Grenfell)

in the 1930s and the subject of automotive engineering was not so big that a dedicated student such as he was couldn't quickly rise to prominence. His reworking gave the car a much more universal appeal, both in practical terms and that vital element in people's cars, personality. He reduced the engine capacity of the 420 Standard from 1193cc to a more than adequate 903cc, especially bearing in mind the dramatic reduction in weight (nearly half a ton) achieved by the incorporation of the new backbone chassis. Under Zubaty's direction this became still lighter, as welded-together girders gave way to a single tubular structure. He also introduced independent front suspension, employing wishbones in conjunction with a transverse leaf. He mounted the new engine on rubber blocks and incorporated the gearbox within the engine housing – an arrangement that would become almost universal more than thirty years later with the widespread adoption of transverse engines and front-wheel drive – again pioneered by Alec Issigonis.

Now the car was ready to take on the world; the legendary 420 Popular was born. Capable of the then heady top speed of 50mph, lighter than any comparable car, frugal on fuel and cheap to buy, it took next to no time to start living up to its name. Here, in 1934, was a real car that would bump-start the motorisation of Czechoslovakia. The Skoda Popular at once represented the acme of Laurin and Klement's dreams and the solid foundation that would establish and sustain the Skoda name down through the next three-quarters of a century of mixed fortunes.

Overhead valves were here to stay. Now they turned up on the 2-litre engine that drove this 1938 Type 923, clearly a larger version of the Popular, and the first car to bear the name Favorit. (Peter Grenfell)

Where once only the headlights and grille distinguished a Skoda from other bases for specialist construction, the move to in-house bodybuilding provided the possibility to give the whole range a family resemblance. Popular, Favorit and the Rapid all share unmistakeable genetic traits. And the similarity is far from superficial. They also share the majority of mechanical components. (Peter Grenfell above; Skoda UK below)

This Rapid from the same year, on the other hand, exhibits little or no family resemblance, clad in its super-streamlined 'motorway' body. (Skoda UK)

All there in black and white. Perhaps not surprisingly, the Skoda Museum has a number of Populars in its collection. The one on the left here is an early Type 418 from 1936, with the original side-valve engine. The one facing us dates from 1939, and is an ohv-engined Type 927. (Peter Grenfell)

This one also dates from 1939 and is listed as a Skoda Popular Roadster 1100. The number refers to the smallest engine offered by that time in Popular derivatives, the 30bhp 1089cc version of the new ohv range, introduced the previous year. (Peter Grenfell)

Enduring popularity. If you needed evidence of the longevity and reliability of the Skoda Popular, look no further than this exquisite 1938 Type 420 Monte Carlo Sport, pictured during the Historic Rally of Bohemia in 2000. (Peter Grenfell)

SIX

WAR AND ITS AFTERMATH

GOING ON TO WAR

By the standards of the time, the Popular was a phenomenal success. Skoda's board was suitably appreciative and all seemed right with the world. So much so that the design team went into overdrive. Between 1934 and the end of the decade there appeared to be no end to the stream of new concepts and prototypes issuing from the now entirely absorbed Skoda studio. Luxury cars were conceived – largely to accommodate the new wave of proselytising Skoda company directors. Microcars were proposed, but these were met with less enthusiasm.

Perhaps the most interesting concept from the period was the rear-engined Skoda 935. Revealed only a year after the launch of the Popular, this represented an entirely different approach to car design. It's hard to say whether anything quite as elaborate as industrial espionage was involved, but the 935 bore more than a passing resemblance to the work of one of Skoda's competitors. Wayward genius Hans Ledwinka – inventor of swing-axle independent suspension – had designed a series of rear-engined cars for Tatra, mainly featuring futuristic aerodynamic body styling and horizontally opposed air-cooled engines. Now, here was the 935 from Skoda, complete with streamlining and a flat engine. It had even been intended for that engine to be an air-cooled diesel, and some development work had been done with prototypes. In the final version, however, the engine was petrol driven and water-cooled and, unlike the Tatra design, was mounted forward of the rear axle.

Ledwinka's practice of fitting the engine in the rear overhang imbued his Tatras with some interesting handling characteristics – especially when substantial flat-six and V8 engines were combined with huge wind-sensitive fins. In fact, members of the German occupying forces, who commandeered Tatras as the local 'prestige' marque during the Second World War, came to regard them as a secret weapon. From all appearances Skoda's car would have been rather more stable and predictable than the Tatra 77, which would have been its direct rival. No action for plagiarism seems to have been forthcoming from Ledwinka and

The most interesting car Skoda never made, this extraordinary device would have had a flat-four air-cooled engine mounted behind the rear axle. Designated 932, it was first revealed in prototype form in 1932, but never entered series production. Other features designed in by Hrdlicka included a hydraulically-operated single dry plate clutch and rack and pinion steering. The whole was based on an innovative backbone chassis, which divided front and rear to carry subframes and engine mountings. (Skoda UK)

Also denied series production, the 935 shared most of its mechanical components with the 932, but looked to its competitor Tatra for styling cues. (Skoda UK)

there were certainly features in the 935 that owed nothing to him – including a fuel tank that fitted into the tubular chassis backbone!

The more conventional Popular went on from strength to strength, becoming available in a number of body variants, including open toppers, station wagons and delivery vans. It was also joined by a slightly more powerful Rapid version and a flagship model called Superb. With the basic formula proven, only cosmetic facelifts were necessary to keep sales going through to the end of the thirties. The last restyling in 1939 marked a move to more integral, aerodynamic styling references.

As had been the practice for a number of years, under the Laurin & Klement banner, Skoda attended the Berlin Motor Show in 1939. As never before, the firm had models to show the world beyond its borders and was keen to make the most of this prestigious international opportunity for exposure. The cars shown that year were part of an unbroken line that had had its origins in a now defunct empire and swelled to its current position during a period of the kind of intense

It seems surprising now that a car with such up-to-the-minute forties styling as this Skoda Superb 4000 ohv would still be relying on a magneto for its electrics. But it's true. Modern electrics were an optional extra. As might be imagined, such a luxurious beast didn't have many takers lining up, its launch having been overshadowed by one of Hitler's. (Skoda UK)

national pride felt by those who came late to the concept of citizenship. Now, new undercurrents were bubbling beneath the surface of political life in the region and, once again, it would be the Central European states which would be the first to be affected by them.

Among the VIP visitors welcomed by Chief Director Hrdlicka to the Skoda stand at Berlin were Dr Goebbels and Adolf Hitler. Within weeks he would receive a less welcome visit from a General Barckhausen, who had been assigned by the occupying German forces to be military leader of the Skoda works. The Nazis had their own plans for the future of the company, including, in August 1939, its absorption into Hermann Goering's Reichswerke.

Inevitably, as the Second World War began to bite, car markets, both domestic and export, suffered – causing many workers to be laid off and great hardship to be experienced by their families. But, as in the previous conflict, the factory soon found new uses for its engineering and manufacturing skills.

OCCUPATIONAL HAZARDS

Before long, of course, the military machine began to make its own demands on factory facilities such as those at Pilsen and Mlada Boleslav. Vehicles were needed for strategic operations, for supplies and back up and for agricultural purposes. Unsurprisingly the Pilsen works was soon back in the armaments business, If they had had a choice in the matter, its directors might have thought twice, following their earlier experiences, but they were no longer their own masters. It's likely, also, that they were more concerned with providing whatever work they could for the loyal and frightened workforce, any of whom could be transported to German labour camps if unable to find work at home.

Car production was much reduced but did not cease altogether. Skoda's first class foundries and tooling facilities also found themselves in demand for servicing outside automotive customers. During the war major components for both Mercedes-Benz and BMW vehicles were manufactured at Mlada Boleslav. Skoda also made wings for Messerschmitts. Skoda's own cars evolved to suit the prevailing conditions. The Superb could afford to be full of luxurious equipment and soft furnishings in peace time. Now it formed the basis for a nearly unstoppable six-wheel staff car, denuded of everything but its inherent brute strength. The Popular went through one last metamorphosis in 1940, when the gearbox moved forward to share the engine casing, like other Skoda designs. In this form the chassis would continue in production, largely unchanged, for another thirty years.

Skoda was also charged with the realisation of Dr Porsche's design for an all-terrain vehicle intended to give the Germans the advantage on the notoriously inhospitable territories at the Russian front. The RSO was his second foray into military vehicle design. An earlier effort, during the First World War, had not distinguished itself. In trials on agricultural land around Mlada Boleslav, attended by the doctor himself, the new creation's fearsome metal wheels ploughed straight into soft ground and obstacles, sticking the vehicle fast. A strangely tolerant Nazi High Command commissioned limited production regardless, and the RSO went on to be a liability on a number of the battlefields of Europe, although no examples ever reached Russia. Ferry Porsche was to find his talents lay elsewhere.

Skoda's wartime masterpiece was based on a Superb top range limo, but took a very different form in military guise. With extremely long travel suspension, the Type 903 Command Car could usually guarantee to have all six wheels in contact with the planet surface, no matter what shape it took. Available with a choice of two six-cylinder engines – the smaller of 2704cc – by far the majority of examples were delivered with the larger, 3137cc unit, delivering 75bhp. The four rear wheels were mounted on tandem swing-axles and shared longtitudinal leaf-springs, so the forward of the two wheels would 'soften up' the one behind for large bumps or declivities. (Skoda UK)

As the war progressed it became clear that, through no fault of its own, Skoda was once more on the losing side. As the Allied grip tightened, raw materials, energy and food began to dry up. Real difficulties faced not only those trying to produce goods, but everyone trying to scratch an existence under the sway of a largely spent force. Like it or not, the Czech economy was dependent upon that of the occupying power. The slow undermining of that power did nothing to improve conditions for the citizens of occupied countries in the short term.

Only thirty Skoda Type 973 four-wheel drives were built, one of which survives at the Skoda Museum. Known affectionately as 'Babeta', it was never commercialised, but did get a supporting role in a contemporary Czech movie. (Skoda UK)

No going back. Still wearing the camouflage paint that didn't save it in the end, this Type 254D was liberated at St Lambert-sur-Dives on 20 August 1944, and now resides in a French museum. Produced between 1935 and 1943, the 254D was Skoda's only diesel wartime lorry, with a four-cylinder engine of 3770cc. Petrol models had a similar cab and driving position, but extended the nose beyond the front wheels to accommodate longer six-cylinder engines, of 2704 and 3137cc respectively. (Simon Fletcher)

The commencement of hostilities meant that even this fabulous (or, should that be fabulously) Superb Cabriolet found few buyers. In total, fewer than 300 Superbs were produced in the period 1938–40. Contrast that with limousine sales of around a thousand a decade earlier. This car boasted a straight-six engine of 3137cc, developing 85bhp and capable of nudging 80mph. It had four-wheel hydraulic drum brakes and synchromesh on the top two of its four forward speeds. (Skoda UK)

PARTY GAMES

On the very day that the armistice was signed, 9 May 1945 – returning Luftwaffe planes mounted a final air raid on Mlada Boleslav, destroying much of the factory and surrounding houses and killing 150 people. This kind of miserable irony was widespread in the aftermath of six years of bloody conflict. Just as the pawns in the political nightmare began to heave sighs of relief, fate had one last cruel trick to play upon them.

Even then the survivors' difficulties were far from over. Reconstruction required not just a will but a plan. People were tired, hungry and nervous about embarking on activities they knew from first hand experience could be curtailed at a stroke. Where only days before the despotic and terrifying rule of the Nazis had been omnipresent, now there was a vacuum. People had lost the habit of making decisions for themselves. They were just looking for a rest from being bossed about by anyone for once, while the dust settled and birdsong returned to the countryside.

But there were pressing matters. If any normality was to return, it wouldn't just be as a result of the decline in abnormality. It would have to be actively recreated. Production, services, agriculture, transport, communications – all these things would have to be re-established, organised and administered. Czechoslovakia's vacuum exerted its inexorable force and in popped the Communist party. If the rule of the Third Reich tended to be arbitrary, that of the new administrators was positively whimsical. Still less wedded to the free market than their predecessors, they arrogated all decision making, large or small, assigning it to unwieldy, often misguided, committees and subcommittees of their ideological brothers.

Still reeling from the last minute air-raids, Mlada Boleslav concentrated on restarting its commercial vehicle production, seeing this as most vital to the reconstruction process. For the moment servicing of whatever market there might be for personal transport could be left to competitors, such as Jawa, whose Minor II was a natural austerity model, and whose production facility had not been touched by the war.

The new political administration had other ideas. In their new plan for co-operation, rather than competition, the only fully operational factory, with the ideal post-war product, would abandon car production and turn over to motorcycle manufacture. Tatra's mass market models would also be discontinued in favour of concentration on its V8 luxury flagship. Czechoslovakia's car market leader, Praga had suffered its own eleventh hour air raid, courtesy of the Americans, but was busily expediting a recovery of its dominance. Then the new bureaucracy delivered a second blow, in its way every bit as explosive and devastating as the first. In common with nearly all of the country's other automotive enterprises, Praga was to relinquish the position it had laboured so long and hard to achieve, and turn its attention to truck-making.

Whatever the reasoning behind all this, it left the way open for Skoda to take over the role of national car maker. Mainly using components manufactured during the war years, Mlada Boleslav was soon able to meet public demand for new cars, which grew as the economy was put back into some kind of shape. Thanks to the machinations of the new administration, the new national motor plan wound up being spearheaded by the Popular which, despite a further cosmetic revision to its bodywork, retained almost all the mechanical elements of the pre-war car.

PROBLEM SHARING

Despite having the field thrown open to their cars, Skoda was not quick to capitalise on the sales potential of the new Popular models. The demand was there, not only on the domestic market but wherever the democratisation of motoring was taking place. The car itself could hold its own with the products of most European manufacturers from either side of the ideological divide. What's more, Czechoslovakia's new controlled economy didn't really generate much income. Many of the vehicles and other products produced domestically were destined for military or state owned customers out of whom it was not easy, or always wise, to make a profit.

The prevailing Marxist-Leninist economic model was oriented toward the redistribution of wealth, rather than its generation. You can only redistribute the same amount of wealth so far before you come up empty-

Looking a bit like an overgrown Renault 4CV in this picture, the Tudor 1101 arrived in May 1946 as a long-awaited replacement for the pre-war Popular. Mechanically it wasn't all that different, although it had a smart new suit of clothes. Like its predecessor, the 1101 would soon become everyone's idea of a basic, practical car. Its 1089cc engine was an ohv unit that drove the rear wheels via the familiar torque-tube. It now had all-hydraulic brakes, synchro on third and top and dynamo-driven six-volt electrics. Steering was by worm and nut and suspension was all independent, by upper-wishbones and transverse leaf at the front, and Ledwinka-style swing arms at the rear. (Skoda UK)

It is interesting that, despite front-hinged doors having been present on the original 420 Standard, front-opening 'suicide' doors were the norm, throughout the production lives of the Popular and 1100 ranges. This long wheelbase version of the 1102 has four full doors (though it would still be referred to as a Tudor) and even finds room for a limousine-style third window at the rear. The 1102 was a slightly updated 1101. Altogether, about 67,000 examples were produced between 1946 and 1952. (Skoda UK)

This beauty dates from 1948 and is preserved at the Skoda Museum. Designated a Tudor Roadster Cabriolet, its curvy body was built, in the Tudor manner, using timber frame construction. (Skoda UK above; Peter Grenfell below)

handed. Motor cars such as the Skoda Popular provided an ideal way to
take some currency off some of the bourgeois capitalists beyond the iron
curtain. If enough examples could only be produced to satisfy demand,
wealth from these other nations could be redistributed Mlada Boleslav's way.
Unfortunately the half-hearted cobbling together of leftovers that passed for
industry at that time was hard-pressed even to meet local orders.

It was not until the beginning of the 1950s that the new economic
models began to bear their own kind of fruit and strengthened production
saw Skoda catching up at last with the exponential growth in private
motoring. The company entered the new decade, still mainly reliant on
the trusty Popular. But after a hiatus that would be inconceivable today, it
also had some new models to offer. Most significant of these was the
1200, the first car from the company whose bodywork wasn't based on a
wooden skeleton. Boasting an up-to-the-minute design with integrated
wings and radiator grille, it brought new levels of power and comfort to
the Skoda range – though, apart from the uprated engine, little else had
changed under the skin.

Although this development helped to further regenerate enthusiasm at
Mlada Boleslav – and at what was now known as the Vladimir Ilyich
Lenin factory at Pilsen – Skoda, like other companies under communist
rule, suffered from being unable to plot its own destiny. Rather than an

One thing that Tatra had done
some time before was dispense
with separate wings, or
mudguards. Now other
manufacturers followed,
including Skoda, who were once
more face-lifting superannuated
mechanicals. The result was the
1200/1201, seen here in four-
door saloon form. With the
familiar engine bored out to
1221cc and the other running
improvements that had taken
place over the years, the 1201,
in its smooth, coherent new
skin, would none the less have
felt very different from the pre-
war Pop. (Skoda UK)

The useful 1200 estate. Both stylistically and mechanically, saloon and estate models were on a par with the products of the majority of western contemporaries. Consider the Hillman Minx, Standard Vanguard, Renault Frégate or Opel Kadett. (Skoda UK)

entity in its own right, it was now regarded as nothing more than a department in a colossal state automotive works that lumped it together with all its erstwhile rivals. This meant that when, for example, it was deemed more important to produce Tatra lorries at that firm's plant in Koplivnice, production of the Tatra 600 saloon was moved, lock, stock and oversteer to Mlada B.

The decision makers didn't stop to think with what mixed emotions workers there would toil upon the production of rival motors. But, if it was unsentimental, the plan could hardly be claimed to be expedient or rational either. The logistics of moving jigs, raw materials, dies, lathes, cranes, parts, conveyors and presses from one factory to another are the stuff of nightmares. Everything that had been working well a week before had to be re-balanced, re-calibrated, re-tensioned. Staff and supervisors at the new factory had to have crash courses in the construction and finishing of the unfamiliar car. The expense of the move and the problems it engendered have probably never been recouped in real terms by Tatra to this day.

The successor of the 600 was also well into the development stage when the decision was made to switch production to Mlada Boleslav in 1951. The so-called Tatraplan was every inch a typical Ledwinka design, completely at odds with Skoda's own developmental path. Although the factory turned out a couple of thousand of the things, it is doubtful if, once the vast eternal plan that brought it thither had been unravelled (if ever it was), there was anything in it for them at all.

The Tatraplan bore no resemblance to existing Skodas. Its very philosophy was different, making it unlikely that its transfer to Mlada Boleslav would be exactly seamless. Based on a frameless monocoque body, it was powered by a flat-four air-cooled engine of 1952cc, mounted longitudinally aft of the rear wheels. Delivering 52bhp to the rear wheels, it gave the slippery-shaped machine a top speed of nearly 80mph. Its aerodynamics also contributed to honourable fuel consumption figures in the high 20s. Steering was rack and pinion and suspension independent – swing arms at the rear being the only common feature with its adopted family. (Skoda UK)

Long after saloon versions were discontinued, commercial variants of the 1200 and 1201 plied the roads of Central Europe. They took as their base this ruggedly competent estate model, tens of thousands of which were sold during its nine years in production. (Skoda UK)

FALSE ECONOMY

The war had been over for the best part of a decade, but workers and ordinary citizens were still waiting for any of the material benefits promised by the new regime to be realised. In fact, those few who had any appreciable assets before that time were worse off, because everything they once possessed had been redistributed to their political masters by means of 'nationalisation'. Even this couldn't buoy up a financial plan out of step with the rest of the world, however. So in 1954 the Czechoslovak crown was devalued by a factor of 5,000 per cent! As might be imagined, this measure was not successful in stimulating a consumer spending boom. Neither did it do much for the domestic car market.

None the less, it was the government's avowed purpose to get the country mobile so, bit by bit, the designers and engineers at Mlada Boleslav edged toward the development of a modern 'standard' car. The car that appeared that year would set the exterior style for the firm's cars for some years to come, and remain indelibly printed on the minds of those of us who first discovered the marque in the 1960s. Mechanically, however, the Spartak was not that different from the Popular or the 1200. Named more with an eye to the 1953 Italian remake than the more famous later US remake, starring Kirk Douglas and Tony Curtis – which was not released for another six years – the car's evocation of the legendary gladiator, Spartacus, was an indicator of its designers' confidence in its ability to take on its task. The bean-counters and paper-shufflers down at party HQ thought the name – any name – smacked a bit too much of personality. In their glorious monochrome vision, everyone and everything was just a number. So Spartak became car number 440.

As a passenger car, the 1200 faded away. A development of it, called 1201, continued to provide the body styling base for various utility vehicles and light commercials. By this device – one of the fifties' management's more inspired ideas – parts produced for the 1200 could be used up while, at the same time, the passenger range became effectively and attractively distanced from its commercial concurrents.

By the end of the decade the 440 had become the 445 and was joined by a number of variants, including the perennially appealing 450 open-topper. In 1959 the old leaf arrangement on the front suspension was at last done away with in favour of coil springs. In honour of this first major mechanical development since the 1930s, proper model names were reintroduced. In place of the soulless numbers, now there were romantic-sounding girls' names. The 445 became Octavia; 450, Felicia – names that would make much more of an impression, both at home and overseas, where, unlike girls' names from some other countries (one thinks of Marjorie, Gladys or Edna), they were just as distinctive and pronounceable.

Where the 1200's styling cues, like those of the Vanguard et al, had been based on truncated versions of the American Dream, the original Spartak made the error of adopting that country's flash to over-clutter a truly compact car. While not as alarming as the even more misguided Standard Pennant, it tended to bracket the car with other fin-encrusted two-tone Eastern Blockers like the Borgward Isabella and the Wartburg 311. (Skoda UK)

In the slightly more restrained single colour of the example housed in the Mlada Boleslav museum the genesis of the later Octavia is clear to see. By the time it entered production the Spartak had become 440/445 Tudor (there's that joke again) and the 450 Roadster. The 440 and 450 models used the proven 1089cc engine, the 445 the larger 1221cc. Power was still delivered to the rear via the torque tube, suspension was still by leaf springs and steering by worm and nut. Speedwise, the car was M1 ready (although it was ahead of its time in being limited to 70mph), and fuel economy was a pronounced improvement at 36mpg. (Peter Grenfell)

The Spartak's curves and grooves tended to camouflage the fact that it was actually a pretty space-efficient design – especially if this publicity picture is to be believed. Before you ask, that's not the spares kit. (Skoda UK)

SEVEN

INTO THE 1960s

A MILLION'S WORTH OF PLEASURE

The sixties were a time of extremes in car design – and dimensions. In Britain, Rolls-Royces, Jaguars, Armstrong-Siddeleys, Standard Vanguards and Humber Super Snipes were huge; Bond Minicars, Nobels, Peel Tridents and the Meadows Frisky were microscopically small. In France, the Renault Frégate was big on avoirdupois, while the 4CV was *mince*.

Most people wanted an ordinary family car. Average performance, average size, but below average money. The Austin A60, the Ford Consul, Taunus 20M, Peugeot 404, Vauxhall Victor and Opel Kadett all fulfilled the first two requirements, but most people couldn't afford to buy them new. Instead, the majority of motorists in the early sixties, throughout Europe, were keeping old cars on the road. Before progressing to a Mk III Vanguard and an A60, my dad drove a 1938 Vauxhall and a 1937 (pre-Sunbeam) Talbot. The latter had 'underslung' leaf spring rear suspension, wire wheels, a side-valve Hillman engine and about 7in of play on the steering.

Even in blatantly and enthusiastically capitalistic regions of the world, such as Paignton, new car ownership was a far-off dream for the majority. But people like Torquay and Newton Abbot car dealer Freddie Hawken had connections to far-off places that could make that dream a reality. In the case of Skoda, the far-off place was Dagenham and that's where, in the company of my dad, I saw my first Octavia. Shrewd operator though he was – bringer to Torbay of Heinkel, Trojan, Lambretta, Reliant and Fiat – Freddie had limited showroom space. With an enviable reputation for shifting specialist marques, he would not have been held to any restrictive franchise obligations by Skoda's importers. So there was no need for transporters. He would have one Octavia and see how it went.

My dad was sent by train to London to drive the thing back. At this distance, I assume Freddie paid his train fare and he paid for mine. Either way, after a journey lasting several hours, involving a change at Newton Abbot and the time-honoured lunacy of crossing London, we arrived at a holding area in Dagenham, where surprising (to me) numbers of Skodas stood alongside the infinite ranks of Fords (no change there). Our Octavia was 'in wax' – a thick coating of protection applied at car factories in

THE OCTAVIA WILL AFFORD THEM A MILLION'S WORTH OF PLEASURE

those days. The practice probably continues, though I haven't seen evidence of it on any recent factory visits. Maybe they use cling-film now. Back then there were no cataphoretic treatments, no galvanic baths. Some manufacturers were lucky to get brochure shots done before rust bubbled through the paintwork. This was not, as I recall, one of Skoda's problems, but the practice of embalming cars was universal, and did, at least, ensure that the rot was suspended until the deal was signed.

Most of the cars Freddie dealt in were lightweight. Heinkel and NSU demonstrated how finesse, coil springs and rack and pinion steering could bring a new aesthetic lightness to the business of motoring, while being just as rugged as the lumbering leaves, cast-iron chassis members and play-inducing worm and nut gears we knew and trusted. The Octavia did not fall into this category.

I recall my father, who had made an earlier living driving ex-War Department lorries for a Marldon haulage contractor (crash gearboxes and no steering assistance), muttering words that were not then considered polite as he piloted the thing through London and out on the Great West Road. Having never been a great traveller, so having only a vague idea of its geographical origins, he made some allusions to the female tractor drivers from the Soviet Union that were the only people from the Soviet Union, apart from Krushchev, we ever saw on British television. However, my father was not displeased by the Skoda's sheer weight and micrometer-busting metallurgy. 'Built like a tank' was high praise at a time when the Morris Oxford was condemned as flimsy and insubstantial because new precision pressing techniques had succeeded in making it light enough to go round corners.

An Octavia advertisement – part of Skoda's 1960s profile-raising in Britain. (Author's collection)

This is where I came in. The Octavia was a toned down Spartak, stylistically more acceptable in Western European circles. Sometime during the run of the 440, synchromesh had crept down to second gear, but otherwise there wasn't much to distinguish the car from its predecessor. Its real significance to the likes of us is that it was the subject of Skoda's first real export drive since the war (the first one), and the first car to bear the name most people the window side of the iron curtain would have seen. The aspirations of many British and European motorists were no different from those in Brno or Ceska Budejovice. If it wasn't Budvar or Pilsner Urquell, Watney's Red Barrel was still beer (just) and the British could recognise an honest bargain when they saw it, too. They saw it in Freddie Hawken's window and there was no going back. Sometimes there was no going forwards either. But Skoda had revealed itself to an enthusiastic corps of disciples who would champion the marque regardless of problems or setbacks. If the worst happened, these stalwarts would not go forward together. (Skoda UK)

The face-lifted Octavia – which lost the ornate bar across its grille. (Peter Grenfell)

The white Octavia saloon drew many interested glances along the seemingly endless A30. There were no motorways, no dual carriageways and no bypasses. We travelled in procession with Standard 10s, Jowett Javelins, Scammell Scarab three-wheeled lorries and the Royal Blue coach. For many of our fellow travellers 0–60 was not even a option. It took some lorries and buses longer to change gear than it would take a present-day diesel Fabia to reach the motorway limit. It was a different world, here as abroad. So it was easier for a car with pre-war mechanicals to make out than modern commentators might imagine. If Octavia's unfathomable arm-wrestling column change had to compete with something light and smooth, it could have been a different story. As it was, even so-called sports cars in the sixties suffered from agricultural changes that would often kick out of gear with enough force to break your shoulder. Similarly, handling characteristics that were a cross between a Hindustan and the *Torrey Canyon* put it on a par with a Daimler Conquest or a Vanden Plas R, both of which were thought to be good.

At root, the car was what a sizeable proportion of motorists needed at that time – and not a few still look for today – an honest family workhorse, with a bit of character and a sense of solidity, a minimum of frills and the least possible outlay. Warranties were good for the time, servicing relatively cheap and, even with purchase tax and import duty, you could buy one for around £600 – a lot less than a Reliant three-wheeler. The Octavia proved such a hit with the citizens of Torquay that Freddie, who had been around long enough to know that the motor trade was all about volume, ordered another one. In a sort of brickpaint red, this was even rarer in its price range, offering as it did estate car practicality to go with its family-friendly two-door body.

Up and down the country, and across the rest of Europe, there were more than enough Freddies to ensure the marque's proliferation. The uncharacteristically efficient party car export agency, Motokov, took stands at international motor shows and commissioned advertisements in national publications, activating prospects and supporting the distribution network.

Back in Czechoslovakia, even sporadic foreign currency sales had a big effect on the economy. The mounting success of the Octavia and its derivatives did much to restore pride and faith in a people deprived of incentive or individual ambition. If it seems at first like an access of unwonted enthusiasm on behalf of the copywriter, the advertising slogan 'The Octavia will afford them a million's worth of pleasure' is an indicator of just how significant the car was in the lives of those who depended upon it. It should also be remembered that, following the devaluation, they had a clearer idea of what a million was worth.

The Octavia had a creditable competition career. Here, an Octavia Super is shown keeping its end up in the 1960 Monte Carlo. (Graham Whyte collection)

No apologies for including this gallery of Felicia pictures. This was a car that brought real class and fun at a knock-down price. In the end only about 15,000 were produced, which is a bit of a tragedy when you look at survivors and reassess the thing's latter-day attractions. (Skoda UK above; Peter Grenfell below)

This Felicia took part in the 1999 Skoda Tour of Denmark. (Peter Grenfell)

When winter set in you could even stick a hardtop on and convert your Felicia into a ravishing coupé. (Skoda UK)

These publicity pics of the Felicia evoke an age of motoring hard to recapture these days, with the benefit of air-conditioning, electronic stability programs and crumple zones. You got cool by taking the top off and getting facefuls of unconditioned dust, stability was a foreign language and everything else would crumple before your Felicia did. We've come a long way since then, but how much of it do we remember? (Skoda UK)

EIGHT

A NEW ERA

TROUBLES LIKELY TO OCCUR

This ominous – and not unfounded – heading is included in the pages of the 1000MB Owner's Manual, along with dire warnings against 'incompetent tampering'. Launched in 1964, this car marked a complete change in design philosophy. Where every other model since the thirties had been a variation on the same mechanical theme, everything about the 1000MB was new. Therein, of course, lay the potential so darkly augured above. A monocoque affair, incorporating front and rear subframes, it had ultra-modern styling and followed a trend fashionable in the sixties by having a rear-mounted engine. Volkswagen, NSU, Fiat – even Renault (Dauphine, R8) and Hillman (Imp) – all led from the rear in those days, and it would have been easy to imagine that such a configuration would be the coming thing. Indeed, both the Dauphine and rear-engined Fiats had proven themselves especially well adapted to the often nightmarish driving conditions then prevalent in Eastern Europe. Government-run automotive divisions had no hesitation in adopting someone else's winning formula – even down to the body styling.

But the 1000MB was no copycat. It was a spacious, practical, four-door saloon that would go on to prove itself in some of the most demanding world rallying events. Like its predecessor, it offered remarkable value for money, but that car's now outmoded tank-like quality had given way to a bit of chic – something altogether more in tune with the swinging sixties. Launch fanfares and advertising support for the new car all did right by it, and its image was further enhanced by its inexorably mounting competition successes.

It is a hard to accept truism when it comes to motor cars that, if they cost little when new, they will be worth next to nothing when you've finished with them. Buying a new budget car might get you off the second-hand treadmill, but it will only really have a trade in value against another budget car. When you think about it, it stands to reason. But many of those who bought Skodas precisely because of their ability to undercut Western European prices, felt let down in some way when they couldn't trade up to a Corsair or a Victor 101.

Owners and traders began to be critical. It was only to be expected that any domestic motor industry, constrained by much higher labour

When the go-ahead was finally given by party central for an entirely new car that would sweep away the antediluvian mechanicals of the Octavia, it came clipped to a wad of conditions. No surprises there, but, rather than going for even thicker metal, the newly issued parameters demanded something as big as the Octavia, but considerably reduced in avoirdupois. That could only mean one thing – a move to monocoque frameless body construction and final goodbyes to the backbone chassis that had been providing the – er – backbone to the company's models in the Kaiser's day. The first product of the new thinking was this prototype, designated 976. (Skoda UK)

Powered by a 900cc front-mounted water-cooled engine, the 976 pre-empted the firm's output half a century into the future, by being the first and last exercise in front-wheel drive prior to the Favorit of 1988. Before the body shape was abandoned a rear-engined version was tried, but both configurations were found to be too confined. (Skoda UK)

Much of the enthusiasm for rear-mounted engines seems to have proceeded from admiration of Renault's Dauphine, which had successfully enclosed its trusty 845cc engine, four doors and five seats into an extremely compact and economical package. Production of the Dauphine had been licensed for some years, so all its little secrets were known to the exploratory surgeons of Mlada B. (Skoda UK)

and component costs, would not be keen on cut-priced imports. But much of the criticism levelled at the cars was based on the fact that they were not what they had never set out to be. Most cars in the 1960s were terribly unreliable by today's reckoning. Production standards at home and abroad could be abysmal. Often loose bolts and connections were discovered and rectified at the PDI (pre-delivery inspection, carried out by dealership mechanics) stage. Just as often they weren't. It's unlikely that Skoda cars were that much worse than the norm, but they certainly were a preferred target for mud-slinging. What's sure is that there will have been teething problems with a design as radically different as this was from what the factory had been engaged upon for so many years. What's equally certain is that the 1000MB, more than any of its forebears, succeeded in establishing a loyal and enthusiastic following for Skoda around the world, from Europe to Australasia, that would stick around long enough to see the company enter its second century as one of the most successfully positioned marques in the automotive world.

The same size limitations that caused the 976 to be abandoned troubled the second prototype to be presented – the Type 977/978. Once again, the same body shape was tried in both front- and rear-engined arrangements. And, once again, the location of the engine wasn't the problem. (Skoda UK)

Coming or going department. These later stages of prototype development were both rear of engine, but looked undecided. In fact, only the essentially forward-facing air ducts at the far end tell you you are not looking at them from behind. Neither saw the light of day, though the lighter, two-tone one gave more than a hint of what was to come. (Skoda UK)

The final production version of the 1000MB was a stylish-looking modern car, even if it did back the wrong horse by going for a rear engine just when Alec Issigonis and Saab were proving that Citroën had been right about front-wheel drive all along. Here was a lightweight monocoque body, larger than the Dauphine, but benefiting from some of its genius – and not inclined to that car's tendency to invert itself in inexperienced hands. The 1000MB was powered by a water-cooled 998cc engine, mounted longitudinally – in established practice – aft of the rear axle. This accounted for the pronounced rear overhang, an echo of the push-me-pull-you prototypes. Power peaked at 42 bhp (later raised to 48) and the car's top speed was in the region of 75mph. All forward gears now had synchromesh and the all-independent suspension was now coil-, rather than leaf spring-based, with an anti-roll bar at the front. Steering continued to be by good old-fashioned worm and nut, but Skoda were by no means the last people to be convinced by rack and pinion. Ford and Vauxhall were still using recirculatory ball and, apart from the Issigonis derivatives (including the Morris Minor and Wolseley/Riley 1.5s), BMC hung their faith on cam and peg in the sixties. (Skoda UK)

This was the publicity department's view of the ideal sixties scene. A forest of high-rises, no other cars in the street – just you, a hat, a dark suit, your loved one, a wig, a fur coat and a Skoda 1000MB. It didn't get much better. Not until you took your hat off, anyway. (Skoda UK)

NO OTHER 4 DOOR SALOON OFFERS SO MUCH FOR SO LITTLE

For £540, the SKODA 1000 MB is a no-pretence sturdy all-rounder. Carries a full family of five in motorway comfort. And at motorway speeds, yet takes the rough with the smooth with rugged independence. Has a big car specification and small car thirst. Take a look at these features—no other car in the Skoda's price range includes these extras at no extra cost: ☐ 5 alternative seating arrangements ☐ fully-reclining sleep-in seats ☐ 4 doors for comfortable entry ☐ child-proof rear door locks ☐ all round independent suspension ☐ quiet, aluminium-block 45 bhp rear engine ☐ cruises at motorway speeds ☐ 40 mpg economy at touring speeds on regular grade petrol ☐ heater and demister standard ☐ twin screen-washer standard ☐ twin sun visors and facia padded for safety ☐ parking and engine inspection lights standard ☐ 4 quarter light ventilating windows ☐ interior locks for boot, bonnet and filler-cap standard ☐ radiator blind and reserve petrol warning light standard ☐ steering-wheel lock standard for added security ☐ choice of six colour schemes
Octavia Combi Estate Car £610 also available

ŠKODA
The new car you can afford to enjoy
1000MB

Write for colour brochures giving full description.
SKODA (GREAT BRITAIN), 150 Goswell Road, London, E.C.1. Telephone 01-253 7441

Advertising concentrated on the affordable price and the lengthy list of 'extras', a term used in its loosest sense. (Author's collection)

SKODA
does you proud

with ten unexpected extras!

The features built into the new four-door Skoda 1000 MB **heater and demister, anti-theft steering lock, twin jet screen washer** *may surprise you—but that's Skoda all over* **Fully reclining sleep-in seats, parking lights, engine inspection light** *The low Skoda price buys a lot of car* **radiator blind, back seats converting to rigid heavy-luggage platform** *Choose Skoda for what it gives you regardless of price* **Reserve petrol warning, under-body weatherproofing** *All this and up to 40 mpg! Skoda is a car to drive proudly — a driving man's car — a family car that's built for comfort.*

SKODA 1000 MB
£590 2. 5. incl. P.T.

Skoda (Great Britain) Limited
SKODA HOUSE, 150 GOSWELL ROAD, LONDON, E.C.1
Please write for illustrated brochure and the name of your local dealer

SKODA COMBI ESTATE
with all the Skoda extras £610.9.4. incl. P.T.
Recommended retail prices.

The Skoda 1000MB was by no means a dog. (Author's collection)

NEW FACES

In 1968 President Dubcek felt the people of Czechoslovakia had earned the right to have more say in their own destiny. He and some other forward-thinking party officials made their thoughts known to their masters, proposing a liberalisation of the country's regulations and the introduction of a limited degree of independent self-government. Indications that their timing was a bit out arrived by return in the form of tanks and heavy armoury, dispatched on the Kremlin's behalf by Warsaw Pact neighbours.

By autumn of that year every administrative department in Czechoslovakia had undergone a number of personnel changes – and that included all automotive divisions. If no specific infraction could be laid at their respective doors, individuals at all levels could not defend the crime of being there. New incumbents quickly set about proving their worth – or, at least, their existence – by changing anything set in motion by their disgraced predecessors. Good, bad or indifferent, all traces of earlier contributions had to be purged, or changed beyond easy recognition.

Much of Laurin & Klement and Skoda's rallying history was unknown in what was still the 'outside world' in the sixties. The 1000MB was the first car to give the marque's name any kind of sporting spin. Regular images appeared in the popular motoring press of Skodas achieving victory in one event or another, and the company was not slow to capitalise on its success in advertising. By the time of the 1969 European Championships, the competition 1000MB had reached the peak of its evolution into a dauntless and highly respected rally machine. (Graham Whyte collection)

The 1000MB became the 110. Then it was joined by the sexy 110R coupé, soon followed by the blazing 120S competition car. The new regime was making a difference, certainly. Their predecessors would not have been allowed to produce cars like these, even if they'd had the cheek to suggest the idea. Whatever they were called, these new models were variations on a theme established by those same predecessors. So, by the time the millionth rear-engined Skoda rolled off the production line, five years later, design philosophy had undergone another about face. Prototypes came in all shapes and sizes over this period, but the one thing they had in common was their difference from established commercial models. Returning to the formula overturned only a decade previously, front engines and rear-wheel drive were the new orders of the day. A glance at developments in the motor industry as a whole confirms the rightness of this. Rear engines had had their day. The engineers at Mlada Boleslav were as aware of it as anyone and were keen to develop their own front engined, front-wheel-drive car in the new mould, started by the Mini and soon to be adopted even by rear-engine pioneers Volkswagen.

But, despite all the mock-ups and design exercises (one of which was by Giugiaro), the money to develop a radically new car was needed elsewhere. That money continued to go up in puffs of acrid smoke from the Slovakian heavy industries that took priority, while the lack of it can been seen in the cars with which the firm was forced to take on the challenge of the eighties. A mock grille gave them the appearance of a front-engined car, but under the skin hardly anything had changed. This was the Estelle, launched in 1976.

The two-door 1000MBX, introduced in 1966. This rather more sporting model had twin carbs, and a pillarless design. (Julian Nowill)

The Skoda 100 was really a facelifted 1000MB, the modernisation of its image largely achieved by the removal of chrome trim. Vinyl roofs may have come and gone, but the seventies was the era of exposed plastic. The days of pock-marked chrome were over – at least for the next thirty years. The effect was to make the 100 look leaner and cleaner, though perhaps less characterful. There were various model designations, from the basic 100 through the up-specced 100L to the 110 and its L, R, S and LS variants. This picture is of a 110S, which, like all 110s, had the larger 1107cc engine, while 100 models continued with the 100MB's 998cc. (Peter Grenfell)

This factory shot from the seventies shows a Skoda 100 body, complete with doors, waiting to be issued with its mechanical elements. When they arrived, they would not be unlike the mechanical elements of the car's immediate ancestors. (Skoda UK)

An extra couple of headlights and an artistically chopped roof resulted in the distinctive 110R coupé, the perfect car to take over the rallying mantle from the more pedestrian image of the 1000MB saloon. Almost 57,000 of these 2+2s were produced separately from other models in the range, at the Kvasiny plant, in a production run that started and ended with the seventies. (Peter Grenfell above; Skoda UK below)

The Skoda 110 was developed into a rally car (badged the 120S), like its predecessor the 1000MB. (Graham Whyte collection)

The 130RS was the rally-bred version of the coupé, which was already being driven in anger before the polite production version appeared in the showrooms. This example dates from 1977 – prior to the introduction of double headlights – and has a 140bhp 1299cc engine with twin Weber carbs and a limited slip diff. Top speed was of the order of 130mph. (Peter Grenfell)

As the seventies gave way to the eighties 110 became 120 (factory designation: Type 742). As had happened with the Popular before it, the rear-engined Skoda hung on longer than designers, engineers and sales personnel would have wished. (Julian Nowill)

None the less, as these pictures by Simon Clarke reveal, the car had, and continues to have, a strong and enthusiastic following. In fact, it's probably true to say that cars from this era form the greater proportion of enthusiast owned and driven classic Skodas. If this doesn't demonstrate the confidence of man in machine, I don't know what would. You wouldn't catch me doing it. This is Simon's 1985 model 120 saloon. (Simon Clarke)

This is what it looked like when he'd finished modifying it. By all accounts, it went the way it looked, too. (Simon Clarke)

The Skoda Owners' Club has a full range of events and support for owners of classic Skodas. Here's Simon Clarke's latest project – a 1988 110 – competing in one of the club's field events. (Simon Clarke)

The 120 series also had a coupé, known as the Rapid, with new independent rear suspension to replace the swing axles that Skoda had stuck with for almost twenty-five years. An increase in engine cooling efficiency, brought about by the introduction of the full front radiator grille (radiator and cooling fan were mounted at the front – remote from the engine), meant that eighties rear-engined models needed no ventilator ducts in the rear wings. This enabled Skoda's designers to come up with a smooth, uncluttered body that looked as if its engine was in the (now fashionable) front. The car was a huge success for Skoda and had an appeal way beyond those faithful to the marque. Over 30,000 were built between 1984 and 1990. (Skoda UK)

Elevated above the vulgar herd. Uncluttered by fashionable ornament and pared down to the sporting minimum. the 120's lines have aged more kindly than many of its contemporaries. (Julian Nowill)

Here's a Rapid belonging to a member of the Skoda Owners' Club, on dry land and following Simon Clarke through the water. (Simon Clarke)

Three modified Skodas, an Estelle and two Rapids, all belonging to members of the Skoda Owners' Club. (Simon Clarke)

There was also a Rapid convertible which, as demonstrated by this Devon-registered example and the Dutch-owned specimen opposite, could be had with or without a Targa-style rollover bar. (Author)

The Rapid's well-equipped dashboard. The quality of the plastic mouldings still wasn't up to western European standards. (Author)

The 130 designation indicates the presence of a 1300 (1289cc) engine, as opposed to the 1200 (1174cc) fitted in the 120. 1984 was the year when the worm and nut turned, at long last, to more precise and responsive rack and pinion steering. (Author)

Suspension continued to be by coil springs, wishbones and anti-roll bar at the front, with semi-trailing arms and coils at the rear. The 110 had ushered in the era of front disc-brakes. On the 130 Rapid they have hydraulic servo assistance and the system has dual backup circuits. (Peter Grenfell)

NINE

LIBERATION AND VOLKSWAGEN

THE STUFF OF LIFE

Things move fast in the motor industry these days, and modern cars are often seen as somewhat soulless by comparison with the so-called 'classics' we tend to bathe in the rosy glow of nostalgia. Much of the reason for this has to do with the increasing complexity of modern cars, which tends to remove them from the comprehension, or at least from the toolkit, of the home enthusiast-mechanic. But, bemoan this change as we might, the motor car approaches, ever closer, the ideals of its founding fathers. The efficiency achieved routinely by the modern internal combustion engine is light years away from that envisaged by its originators. Qualities of ride, handling, accident management, construction, rust protection, reliability, electrics – all have improved a thousandfold in the last half of the last century; and there is no indication that automotive development will slow down, or take any very surprising new paths, in the coming years.

If you are fortunate enough to visit a modern car factory, you might be bamboozled at first by the apparent automation into missing the vital art, the genius, the engineering excellence and the sheer logistics that only humans could ever, and can still, supply to the process. What you see a robot doing now, a human did first. Computer-aided design (CAD) has made life easier and enabled vastly improved space management, but it works to 'aid' a human, and the computer itself was conceived, built and programmed by humans. My point is that soul is not lacking just because we don't perceive it.

This has particular relevance to the Skoda Favorit, a car now largely dismissed, even by a number of the Skoda faithful. It lost, for them, the quirkiness of the rear-engined years, which found a ready resonance with people whose own characters were determinedly individual. But it didn't quite fulfil the role of international standard bearer. In truth, though, it was vital to the survival of both the company and Czechoslovakia as a whole. As unprepossessing as it has become fashionable to view it, it was a stupendous achievement, born in the most adverse of circumstances. What's more, it wasn't a bad car.

After decades of frustration and disappointment, the engineers at Mlada Boleslav could be forgiven for doubting the first suggestions that permission had been granted, at last, to develop a new, front-engined, front-wheel-drive Skoda. All previous projects had curled up and died and, only months before, party central had published a ludicrous plan to tandem-produce a Russian-designed people's car at plants all over Eastern Europe – including those of Skoda. Now, though the order had been awaited so long, nobody acted upon it. No one really knew where to start or, indeed, whether to start. Skoda had no proper design studio; no one to co-ordinate the new parts or pressings that would be required. Even more bafflingly, in their enthusiasm party central had decreed that the new car would have Italian styling.

Communist-run Czechoslovakia, with its devolved responsibility, idiosyncratic economics and permanent climate of fear and suspicion, was not in the habit of approaching rich and flamboyant Italian car designers. How would they go about it? Could they even afford it? Giugiaro, who had done some advance work for them in the past, turned them down cold. Various others were consulted, with similar results, but Bertone seemed to have a special affinity for the project and even agreed to begin work while still waiting for the lumbering party machinery to come up with a contract. This was just as well, because the decree that authorised the new model also demanded unquestioning compliance and set a delivery date only two and a half years away. Most motor manufacturers would expect a minimum of double that time – and they would expect to call upon the benefits of research departments, design studios, trialling lines and test tracks. The complex processes of siting major components, developing chassis dynamics and containing all the million and one things that make a modern car within a body shape that needs to grow from liaison with a distant stylist are complicated enough. When your budget rules out major restylings, and you have no time to spare, it becomes something else. In the end, it seems probable that the thing would have failed, and heads would have rolled, but for three main factors.

The first was the Skoda board's success in persuading Petr Hrdlicka, son of the pre-war director, to mastermind the project. Like his father, he was a man of principle and integrity, neither of which quality endeared him to party officials, or them to him. As it was, he had to make a major ethical decision to put the project before his abhorrence of the existing administration. He also made his consent to take charge conditional on demands that normally would not be tolerated – including the removal of state-appointed personnel. He was, however, the right – and possibly the only – man for the job, as the success of the venture was to prove.

The second factor was Bertone's extraordinary enthusiasm and flexibility. A top designer, who commanded respect and monumental fees from the biggest and best in the world, he gave the Favorit an entirely disproportionate amount of his time and attention.

The third unlikely factor was the role played by home-grown design leader, Jaroslav Kindl. Kindl had worked with Giugiaro on the seventies designs that never made it. As the most skilled and able car designer in the country, he had done his own studies for the new car – even producing maquettes and full-scale mock-ups in the metal. In a meritocracy, with its own national identity and self-determination, the job of designing the Favorit would have been his. When it went, as part of the official decree, to one of the Italian design houses, he reasonably might have become disillusioned in a big way and flounced off. If he had done so, Mlada Boleslav would have been in serious trouble. No one else in the country even spoke the same language as Nucio Bertone – and I don't mean Italian. If Kindl hadn't agreed to act as liaison between the factory and the great man, it certainly would not have been possible for Skoda engineers to complete running prototypes in less than half of the twelve month period allocated in the plan.

So, when you are looking at a Favorit, you are looking at something of a miracle: an honest, practical, modern, front-wheel-drive car that was produced in half the time it would take any of the world's major manufacturers, by people with no specific training or experience, working in decidedly non-optimum conditions. And, if you stand it next to some of the other cars in the same category from the late eighties, it doesn't look or feel out of place.

I enjoyed the Favorits I road tested at that time for what they were. And what they were, above all, was honest. Their price, their practicality, their big doors and upright seating, their clear controls and their lack of airs and graces suited a big lump of the buying public – the non-car-obsessed necessitous motorist. But my real respect for the car (and other Skodas) came when we toured the newly independent Czech Republic in the early nineties.

I'm late! I'm late! The front-wheel-drive Favorit, with its Bertone styling and radically new design, comes bustling through the Bohemian forest. (Simon Clarke)

Despite the time, physical and financial strictures under which it was developed, the Favorit shares its predecessors' taste for competition. Its transversely mounted 1289cc engine drove the front wheels and was the first to receive what a brochure described as 'pointless' ignition (there's such a thing as asking for it!). This was actually Bosch Motronic electronic ignition with fuel injection. It was also the first Skoda to come with a three-way catalyser. Top speed was just over 90mph and fuel consumption was in the mid-40s. Rack-and-pinion steering was retained and suspension moved to the Eurostandard McPherson struts at the front, with trailing arms and torsion bar, with the addition of coil springs, at the rear. (Peter Cracknell)

By the time of Felicia, the stylised form of the Skoda flying arrow had been long established. Under Volkswagen it acquired its present shade of green and a black surround bearing the words 'Skoda Auto'. (Peter Cracknell)

Those requiring additional carrying capacity could specify a useful estate version for the same money as the hatch. (Peter Cracknell)

This two-door prototype based on the Favorit never made it to production. (Julian Nowill)

When a country is liberated, it doesn't instantly fill up with Golfs and Astras. Skodas had existed before Communism; they had held the country together through the dark times and now they were providing the motive power of the new freedom. Everywhere you looked, in cities, in towns and villages, and in the countryside and forests; in the rapidly reawakening Czech landscape and the still medieval corners of Slovakia's Carpathians and High Tatras, Skodas were delivering the mail, bringing the doctor, providing the life-blood of the community. It is easy in a land of plenty to be smug and patronising. Here are lands that know what hardship means where our choices were unknown, where you could not buy ten different versions of anything you wanted and where your neighbour could be your executioner. In those circumstances, the visionaries, the designers, the engineers and the problem solvers of Mlada Boleslav managed to create machines that would not only service a nation, but draw vital currency from the forbidden lands beyond it. Some joke, huh?

Peter Grenfell came across this Favorit Qualitaire 135 Limited Edition Estate. Production was limited to two hundred, and in 1994, when it was bought, it was the most expensive Skoda model at £8,100. Among its high equipment specification was a eight-speaker stereo and alloy wheels. When photographed, this example had done 86,000 miles, including three trips from the UK to the Czech Republic. (Peter Grenfell)

FELICITATIONS

As the last vestiges of the old dictatorship evaporated in the heat haze of 1989's 'Velvet Revolution', the roads of Central Europe were thronged with foreign investors beating a path to the newly formed Czech Republic's door. In boardrooms and in the exquisitely preserved art nouveau cafés of Prague, plans were discussed and deals signed that would quickly bring the new country into the fold and drench its citizens in the divine light of capitalism. Some of them, anyway.

What nobody from either side of the negotiations knew at the start was exactly how far out of step the republic would be after the best part of half a century of being separated from the pack. But, as audits, inventories and feasibility studies were completed, it became clear that its situation was superior to that of most other Eastern Bloc nations. Romania, for example, or Albania and Bulgaria – even the neighbouring Slovakia – all were still positively medieval by comparison. What's more, the Czech Republic had suffered very little from either war damage or insensitive Soviet building programmes. Though, like Slovakia's capital, Bratislava, Prague had acquired a forest of tombstone concrete blocks of flats, at least they were hidden from view of the great city. The beauty of the timeless capital was to draw tourists from all over the world, film companies and the planet's youth, all converging to fund a new renaissance and to create a trendy new focus for art and culture.

Like many of the Republic's other enterprises, Skoda wasn't in bad physical shape, but its financial health was woeful. The mammoth investment made in the Favorit project still had to be paid back. Under the prevailing system, almost all the proceeds from sold cars were creamed off before the factory got a piece. Besides, in global terms, Skoda was small fry. It might have had the only liberated automotive products able to stand alongside western competitors, but the company itself was in no such position. It was clear that a partner was needed, both to provide investment and to elevate the Skoda brand to the main stage.

There were a number of candidates, among which the most serious were General Motors, Renault and a certain well-known German concern. Renault's plan was a good one on paper. It would supply the vital investment, ensure a speedy move to modernised production processes and guarantee employment. On the other hand, the plan was entirely Renaultcentric, in the sense that there was no talk of new Skoda designs. Activity would have been based around the old eastern bloc standby of building new cars with second-hand tools and dies – the Renault 18, in this case. A nice bonus for la Régie, who would otherwise have had to scrap all that old stuff, and a nice cheap facility in which to build the new Twingo. At that point nobody was entirely convinced this original concept would be anything like the success it turned out to be.

Volkswagen's plan was much better. It involved serious investment, but it respected Skoda's engineering heritage and provided for an altogether more symbiotic relationship. A new Skoda model within five years, designed and developed in-house, was written into the deal. The level of inward investment enabled Mlada Boleslav to update and upgrade all existing facilities as well as installing new plant and technology. Better still, it allowed for development of state-of-the-art engines that could keep pace with anti-pollution legislation. The clincher was that the deal was

The arrival of the Volkswagen group signalled a proliferation of models, equipment and engine options. The new Felicia didn't just turn the same three capacity variations of the same engine to face Wolfsburg. Buyers could now choose from two 1289cc and one 1598cc petrol engines. For the first time, they could also specify an 1800cc diesel engine. (Skoda UK)

not all one way. Volkswagen did not look upon Skoda as a lame duck that needed baling out. It had other metaphors to mix. Rather, it saw Skoda's engineering heritage as a firm foundation upon which to launch future flagships. By the end of the eighties German engineers and designers were already mightily expensive. The reunification and its attendant revaluation of the Deutschmark had made them the more so. In return for all the benefits of Volkswagen family membership, Skoda could bring fractional development costs – so everyone was, and continues to be, happy.

The Felicia arrived in 1994 and marked the beginning of a slow, but inexorable, turnaround in Skoda's world image. In that year, a mere five years on from the company's emergence, it was awarded the ISO2002 designation by the German TÜV testing agency – an indication of the quality and consistency of its products. It would be naïve in the extreme to imagine this award owed nothing to the period prior to the Volkswagen deal. Its coincidence with the completion of the one millionth Favorit was more than enough reason for some long-overdue celebrations in Mlada Boleslav.

Similar in most respects, the estate version of the Felicia retained the Favorit's torsion bar and coil rear suspension, while the saloon gained an independent trailing arm set-up with an anti-roll bar. All the modern features introduced on the Favorit were retained and, despite the PR-ofusion of Volkswagen references, just about everything about the car was what Skoda were doing already. (Skoda UK)

Sense of Fun. Skoda's designers hadn't had much to laugh about since the Tudor two-door riot, so they celebrated the injection of Volksgeldt by creating this little number in canary yellow. Fun by name and nature, it was one of a rash of leisure-oriented vehicles that caught public imagination in the crepuscule of the last millennium. (Author)

Intended as a mount for surfers and those among us who are going to be a model, the Fun combined pickup cred and practicality with the ability to pose up to four people, during the summer month(s). Its brilliance lay in the way the rear seats were incorporated in the rear wall of the cab, where they remained both secure and dry, and did not encroach upon the loadspace. When required, they could be unfolded to provide open air seating, while still leaving room for scuba tanks, a rubber ring, or other adjuncts of the nautical lifestyle. The irony is that most Fun buyers took it rather more seriously. Its dual-purpose design made it perfect for self-employed builders and jobbing gardeners, who only needed to move bodies about at the weekends. Demand (among the limited numbers imported) was high enough that it soon became unnecessary to kit the wife's mother out in sou'wester and oilskins, when Truckman devised a dedicated detachable hardtop that would accommodate the Fun's rear seat mechanisms. (Skoda UK)

The clever sliding rear seats. (Skoda UK)

The Fun's neat dashboard – a huge advance over that of the old rear-engined cars, even if the steering wheel is a step too far in colour co-ordination. (Author)

Despite having an interior colour scheme based on the wasp, the Fun shares the Felicia's rally response rates and surprisingly supple ride. (Skoda UK)

A HUNDRED YEARS ON

With the arrival of the entirely new Octavia in 1996, Skoda's position in the mainstream of global motor manufacturing was confirmed. Every bit as good as equivalent models from its adopted brethren, here was the car that should silence forever the hollow laughter of ill-informed mockers. In the five years since launch it has proven to be exceptionally reliable and well built. It figures high on many motoring journalists' popularity lists (including this one), largely for its sheer ease of use and willingness.

Even with the increasing standardisation of controls and equipment that has occurred, especially in European cars, over the last decade, few vehicles fall so easily to hand as the Octavia, Variants such as the amazingly inexpensive RS Sport and the supremely competent 4×4 mean that there is a model for all occasions – all of which are highly specified and offering a sense of class at odds with erstwhile public perception of the name. But, for all that, the Octavia is very much a Skoda, in the sense that it is an honest car, without unnecessary frills and furbelows, to the extent that, in many people's eyes, the turbodiesel estate is the most desirable model. Only slightly silly TV presenters and the otherwise immature are terribly concerned with reaching 60mph on the public highway in anything much under twelve seconds. The diesel Octavia is quick enough and its top speed easily fast enough, but it is also comfortable, spacious and self-possessed on the road.

It is often revealing to drive a car in its native land and piloting an Octavia TD Estate from Prague airport to the Skoda Museum at Mlada Boleslav gave me an additional dimension on the car. Its uncommonly good visibility, its surprisingly tight turning circle for a front-wheel drive, transverse-engined layout, its ready power and the combination of responsive handling and forgiving ride make it even more impressive in the face of the Czech Republic's tramlines, potholes, cobbles and adverse cambers than I had already found it to be here and in France.

Touring the new factory in Mlada Boleslav increases respect for the car still more. Where a factory of this vintage anywhere else in Europe would have been almost entirely robotised, here are people in large numbers. The still economic Czech workforce ensures that Octavia (and its top-of-the-range leather and veneer variant, the Laurin & Klement) are close to being hand-built cars – at least where it matters. Doors and tailgates are hung with a rare attention to detail. Headlining, upholstery and trimming are done by proper skilled workers, operating in an unusually calm and happy atmosphere. How much more different could it be from the dark days of dictatorship and the merchants of fear?

Just over a hundred unbroken years since Laurin and Klement went into production we were invited to Portugal to try a new compact Skoda model, to be known as the Fabia. The roads around Faro and the medieval streets of the town itself provided a perfect testing ground for the new motor, which endeared itself to us right away, especially for its use of space and its chassis refinement. Shortcomings in Volkswagen Group engines existing at the time were soon resolved, making the Fabia one of the most competent and most modern small cars on the market. Like the Octavia, it is an easy car to get to know. And, also like the Octavia, it is now offered in a wide

This was the first Octavia I road tested. Right from the start, the car's dynamics and build quality impressed. Engines have improved dramatically since then, but the design, driver ergonomics and overall packaging of the Octavia were so right at launch that it seems to have become a classic in the short time it's actually been with us. (Author)

If anything, the Estate version is even more user friendly. Having first driven the turbodiesel version in Prague, I later took one to France. On both occasions, it was the fact that I felt at home so quickly in it that impressed. Diesel also delivers a workmanlike quality to the car that endears it to some of the most spoiled motoring journalists. When one of these was the long-term test car at a certain well-known motoring magazine, there was a race every night for its keys. (Skoda UK)

Benefiting from Skoda's extensive rallying experience with Octavias, the RS, launched in 2001, set the roadgoing whizzer market on its ear. Here is a motor that not only performs, but does so with grace and consummate ease. Now you can have a sporty saloon that doesn't shake your teeth out on the rough and doesn't drive you to distraction in town centres. Despite excellent grip and sporting dynamics, the Octavia RS rides like a grown-up's car. Actual dynamic suspension tuning has been used to achieve the compromise, rather than just hard springs. Likewise, the 1781cc 20v dual-ohc engine knows how to behave when not giving it the whole 180 bhp. Most cars in this category are so tiresome in town that you'd sooner take the bus. Not so the Octavia RS, which has the flexibility, the gear ratios and the refinement to speak only when spoken to. (Skoda UK)

range of variants with a good choice of engines. Build quality and reliability seem excellent and fuel economy is exemplary, though current versions are a bit heavy on the interior plastic. None the less, the Fabia is another solid guarantee that Skoda is more than capable of mixing it with the big boys in the cut-throat car market of the new millennium.

You couldn't have much more of a vote of confidence in the marque than the decision to re-enter the luxury car market with the new Superb. This is a sector in which even the most confident majors get a bit jumpy. Although it wasn't always the case, the widespread tendency in executive and county circles is toward buying what impresses, or intimidates, the neighbours. In this cause labels are everything, quality and suitability to purpose almost irrelevant by comparison. If an otherwise identical Mercedes was re-badged 'Acme' and offered for ten grand less, no traditional Merc buyer would touch it.

Nevertheless, it is not completely impossible to infiltrate the smart set, as Toyota has demonstrated with Lexus. It might be more difficult for names with an already established public image. Conversely, it might get easier as die-hard name droppers give way to new generation scions with the confidence to fly their own colours. After all, Audi came back from the grave. Why shouldn't Skoda? They started making posh motors a very long time ago and some of the Superbs from the past were exactly what they said they were. The new car benefits from all the latest gizmology and is perfectly placed to draw on the accrued mystique of its German parent – a company which, it should be remembered, began by making a rather impractical, underpowered car for the masses.

If, twenty or thirty years ago, you needed a very good reason to buy a Skoda, now it's not so easy to come up with a good reason not to buy one.

Like the RS, the 4x4 is a revelation – not because, like other VW Group excursions into the art-form (4Motion and so forth) it makes a song and dance about being four-wheel drive. More, because all-round traction is the ultimate expression of its general competence. You can tell they got the transmission right, because you're not aware of it. The car just goes where you want it to, There's none of the alarming lurching and twisting that accompanies close relations. It's just all Octavia, only more so. The engine is that of the RS, slightly reconfigured to turn in 150 rather than 180 bhp. The transmission arrangement is permanently engaged via a Haldex coupling, which increases load on the rear driving wheels as required, with the front ones doing most of the work most of the time. Claimed top speed is 131 mph – and they surely wouldn't bother with the '1' if it wasn't true – and combined fuel consumption figures of around 30mpg are acceptable, if you use the four by four enough to justify it. (Skoda UK)

This was the first Fabia I drove at the launch event in Portugal. The view below is taken opposite the Moorish stronghold at Silves. The car featured the 1.4 litre 16-valve engine, and was one of the first we had driven with a drive-by-wire electronic throttle. Its competence in the medieval town centres and challenging mountain roads endeared it to us immediately, though we were less thrilled with throttle response and the superfluity of dashboard plastic. (Author)

This was our favourite car at launch, It was powered by a not terribly refined 1896cc diesel. Although it sounded a bit old fashioned, it responded well and gave the reassuring impression of being one of those cars that would run like clockwork for many years. For such a small car 1.9 litres sounds more than enough, but it was nicely torquey and lazy, making it easy to appreciate the Fabia's other virtues. (Author)

The Fabia's interior fails to reflect the originality of the car's external styling. Only the two-tone colours relieve the monotony of a dashboard in serious need of plastic surgery. (Skoda UK)

Boot camp. There are some people who prefer saloons to hatchbacks, so Skoda recently introduced this odd-looking variant. (Skoda UK)

There is also this happy and practical estate derivative, which offers even more practicality, while being more sympathetic to the car's established personality. (Skoda UK)

A Superb ending to the story so far. In April 2002 Skoda opened its new factory at Krasing in the Czech Republic to produce its new saloon – on the site of the works where the original Superb was built. By re-entering the luxury car market, Skoda demonstrates a confidence in its ability to silence any straggling doubters. More than this, it strikes a telling blow for continuing independence of movement and the true nature of its standing within the Volkswagen Empire. With a predominantly modern, highly competent product range, running from an entry level Fabia to an all-singing, all-dancing Superb, Skoda is perfectly placed to embark on its second century. (Skoda UK)

The Superb's interior is claimed to be the most spacious in its class. Sober suited and on its best behaviour, Superb comes with a wealth of innovative details, and is not devoid of the spirit of eccentricity that marked out its forerunners. No other car in this (or any) class has a secret compartment for an umbrella. (Skoda UK)

TEN

COMMERCIALS

FARE AND SQUARE

Skoda's contribution to private motoring in Czechoslovakia and beyond has been more than equalled by its vital contribution to public transport. In a country where, for most of the last century, the independence of car ownership was far from the norm, the organised movement of people and the removal of their supplies and belongings was an essential to the survival of society.

Skoda buses and commercials would make a book on their own, though mechanically they were drawn from the passenger cars dealt with in this book. In essence, they followed the designs and trends that dictated the forms of such vehicles worldwide, and were often bodied by outside firms, who treated one chassis much like another. Like the Cammell coaches in the UK and the early Setras in Germany, there were exercises in aerodynamic extravagance, but the greater majority were honest, squared-up buses, such as the following, that made the maximum use of the area available to them.

This is a Skoda Type 154, powered by a 1944cc four-cylinder engine, shared with the 4R passenger car. Produced from 1929 to 1931, it was available with a variety of bus, ambulance and commercial bodies. (Skoda UK)

Skoda held patents to the Martin system of articulated semi-trailers, so used the arrangement for military vehicles, commercials and large capacity buses, such as this Type 550 long-distance coach. Engine for this was a four of no fewer than 6786cc. This specific model was designated 550N, and was intended solely for bus use, featuring, as it did, reduced ground clearance and 'comfort' spring ratings. (Skoda UK)

The 505 was larger than the 154, designed to carry more people further. Its engine was a 4,7 litre four and it ran on double wheels at the rear. (Skoda UK)

CARRY THAT WEIGHT

In any industrialised consumer-based society, the movement of goods is a primary area of interest to vehicle manufacturers. Both Laurin & Klement and Skoda produced commercials to suit every need, from light vans to huge logging wagons, from pickups to tankers.

At this time pickup and Forman van versions of the Felicia comprise the company's only commercial offerings, though this might be expected to change in the near future, even if only in the form of a Sevel-type shared presence in the market-place with other Volkswagen Group members.

As described earlier, Skoda's heavy lorries department withered away when the party line lottery picked Tatra as the national truck-maker. But it is to be hoped that the otherwise unbroken line of dependable commercials that kept the country's supplies going throughout the various political and economic vicissitudes will be renewed and revitalised before the Felicia derivatives are no more.

The light commercial market is a particularly important one at this moment in automotive history and Volkswagen's share of it is not all it might be. How much of this is due to cost, how much to greatly improved competition and how much to design shortcomings is hard to say. The present Transporter has chassis dynamics superfluous to delivery van requirements. It is accordingly too expensive, and its body design is not really space efficient. On the other hand, the LT is built from the same panels as the hugely successful Mercedes Sprinter, but doesn't get a fraction of its sales. Perhaps the appearance of an honest, competitively priced, Skoda light commercial is what the world at large, and VW in particular, is waiting for.

What must have been one of Laurin and Klement's most singular projects was designing buses and vans for use in Montenegro. The climb from the Bay of Kotor to the capital, Cetinje, is more than a match for modern vehicles, so it was a very serious challenge in 1909. When we travelled up it in the mid-eighties, we were told that the Austrian engineer who built the road was in love with a Montenegrin princess, whose name began with an M, so he added two more serpentine bends to represent the initial, making twenty-five in all. When 40ft modern coaches take visitors up to the Biljarda Palace – so called because it had the first billiard table in Montenegro – which, incidentally, had to be borne thither by donkeys, prior to the building of the Austrian's road – both front and rear

overhangs live up to their names by swinging across fresh air on a number of the corners. Laurin and Klement's award-winning design featured a high forward-control cab with very easy access and good visibility. The 4562cc four-cylinder engine was mounted under the cab and delivered 28bhp to the rear wheels by way of a curious reverse chain drive arrangement. (Skoda UK)

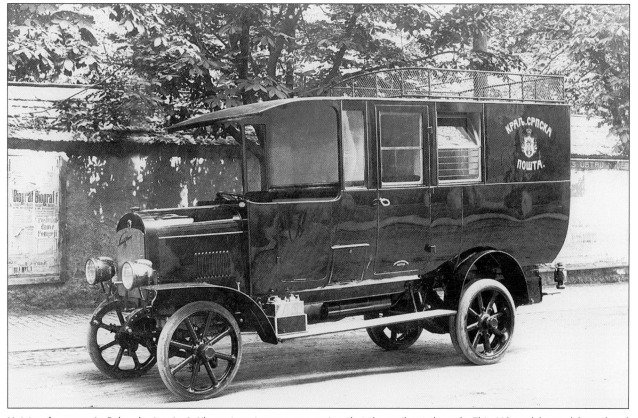

Not too far away, in Belgrade, Laurin & Klement post vans were seeing that the mail got through. This MS model was delivered and photographed shortly before the Serbian capital, and soon the whole world, were caught up in the events of the First World War. Motor vehicles needed to be tough and reliable to cope with conditions here and in Montenegro and the other neighbouring places that would one day comprise the former Yugoslavia. Prague summers can get pretty warm, but they're no match for the blazing heat in the Neretva Valley. Blazing dusty roads across the barren karst can be daunting still. I've seen lorry drivers doing their own major repairs by the roadside because of the impossibility of towing or recovery. Far below the whiplash coast road from Dubrovnik to the mouth of the Neretva, the sun glints off the busted ruins of all the Yugos that didn't make it. You needed to be fearless to launch yourself far beyond the city walls in 1914, and you had to have a fair degree of faith in your trusty Laurin & Klement. (Skoda UK)

It wasn't long before the MS itself was doing service in the war effort. These canvas-covered flat bed trucks were awaiting delivery to the front. MS models were powered by four-cylinder engines of 4713cc, capable of supplying up to 38bhp. (Skoda UK)

The Martin system was much exploited by Laurin & Klement, as here on a Type 646 tractor unit, which is not only pulling the articulated semi-, but a further trailer behind that. Its spoked wheels give it a somewhat flimsy appearance, but this is certainly deceptive, as, it seems, is the impression that it would get bogged down at the first sign of mud. The light, thin wheels and long travel suspension made these old lorries surprisingly agile in rural environments – at least until you got caught in the ruts of a cart track. (Skoda UK)

Contraptions like this 504 from 1923 were used for transporting water, either from place to place, or for washing the highway. Note that there was no weather protection for the driver or his mate. The 504 shared its engine with the MS. (Skoda UK)

And what did you do if your Laurin & Klement should happen to break down? Just what you'd do now, if you were lucky enough to find one of these breakdown lorries. This a Type 125 from the late twenties picking up a casualty in Prague. (Skoda UK)

While Laurin & Klement were already establishing a reputation for their original lorries and commercials, Skoda had acquired the right to build the British Sentinel Steam lorry under licence. One of the most immediately recognisable classically elegant designs from the early years of commercial vehicle history, the Sentinel worked mightily hard for its living in much of the world. Not given to sudden movements, it was none the less extremely strong and powerful, and ideally suited to working in tandem with steam rollers during the worldwide explosion in roadbuilding that was occurring in the twenties. It was also strangely popular with coal merchants. (Skoda UK)

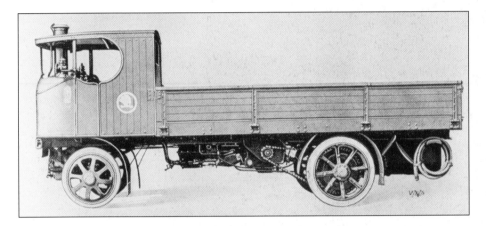

Domestic appliance. L&K and Skoda vehicles were present in all areas of road transport and services. The availability on the home market of reliable commercial bases quickly led to the production of their own fire engines and emergency service vehicles. (Skoda UK)

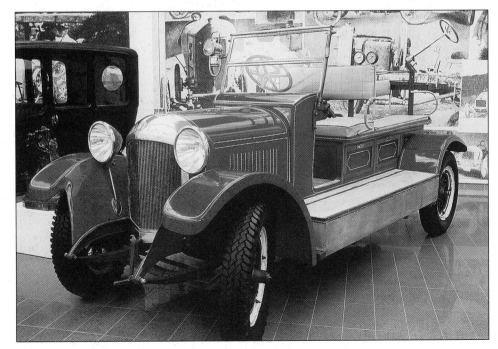

Over the next ten or twenty years the design of commercials worldwide didn't alter that much, with development soon giving way to the sheer demands of peacetime construction, followed by the advent of the Second World War. Skoda lorries tended to retain the same cab and front wheel arrangement, extending the wheelbase to achieve larger load capacities and extending the nose to accept bigger, six-cylinder in-line engines when needed. (Skoda UK)

By the beginning of the sixties, they could afford to be a bit more inventive, and a number of prototypes emerged from Mlada Boleslav, such as this Type 998, aimed at farmers and bearing a remarkable resemblance to the little Haflinger, designed for Austria's Steyr-Puch by Ledwinka. (Skoda UK)

When the 1200 series cars were cut off in their prime by the arrival of the Spartak, their mechanical and spiritual essence survived them in the form of various rather nice vans and pickups in the American mould. (Skoda UK)

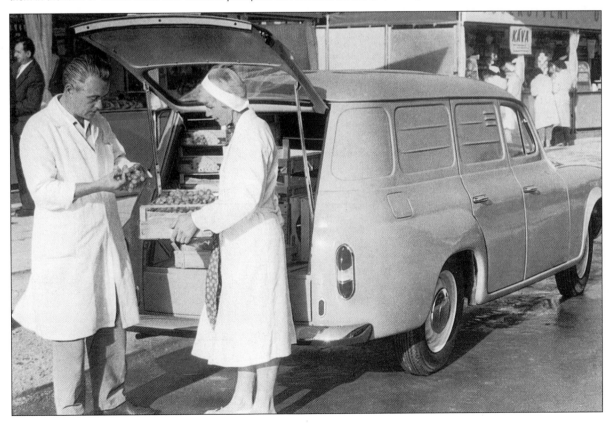

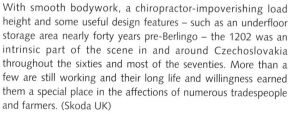

With smooth bodywork, a chiropractor-impoverishing load height and some useful design features – such as an underfloor storage area nearly forty years pre-Berlingo – the 1202 was an intrinsic part of the scene in and around Czechoslovakia throughout the sixties and most of the seventies. More than a few are still working and their long life and willingness earned them a special place in the affections of numerous tradespeople and farmers. (Skoda UK)

Beating even the 1202's record, the forward control 1203 first saw the light of day as the 997 in 1961. With few modifications (a facelift in 1968), it remained in service until 1981. When we visited the newly established Czech Republic, it was the van that did all the things vans do in that country. It also occupied the position an Espace or Space Cruiser would have filled in Western Europe, with various seated and windowed forms supplementing the complete range of commercials – which included most of the country's ambulances; and hearses. Its 1221cc engine was mounted fore and aft, directly above the front wheels and drove the rear in the conventional way. Unusually for a delivery van of the period (other than Citroën's H Van and C32/C35), 997 and 1203 had all-independent suspension, by wishbones at the front and the ubiquitous swing arms at the rear. Produced fairly cheaply, largely by making use of outmoded parts from the passenger car model range, it was the dead right light commercial for its time and place. Its part in seeing the country – and others beyond its immediate borders – through strange and difficult times is inestimable. But both its longevity and versatility cannot but command respect from anyone with a soul. (Skoda UK)

ELEVEN

A CENTURY OF MOTORSPORT

In 1901 Laurin and Klement first began to compete in motorsport, winning the first event they entered, the 1901 Paris–Berlin motorcycle race. The company moved into car racing in 1911, and went on to win such prestigious events as the 1914 Targa Florio in Sicily. In 1925 Laurin and Klement's company became part of Skoda, which continued to focus on motorsport. In 1936 Skoda entered its first Monte Carlo Rally, finishing second in class. In 1948 three Tudor 1101s finished the Spa 24-Hour race and a Tudor Sports model competed in Le Mans in 1950. From then until the end of the 1980s opportunities for competition were severely limited by the political environment, but Skoda continued to compete wherever it could, including the European Touring Car championship.

It was in rallying that Skoda earned its reputation, however. Cars modified in the factory and tuned by enthusiastic drivers were entered into rallies throughout Europe during the sixties, seventies and eighties. Rugged rally cars, including the 130RS and the Bertone-designed Skoda Favorit used their legendary grip to score countless victories, including class wins on World Championship events such as the Monte Carlo, 1000 Lakes, Acropolis, San Remo and the British RAC Rally.

Skoda's partnership with Volkswagen in 1991 heralded a new beginning for Skoda, including the creation of an in-house competition department, Skoda Motorsport. In the 1992 season Skoda Motorsport won their World Rally Championship class eight times. Better was to come in 1993, when Skoda won the inaugural FIA F2 World Championship for 2-litre cars, their 1300cc Favorits trouncing the 2-litre entrants. Skoda Felicia Kit Cars were introduced in 1995, with more class victories and Stig Blomqvist's stunning third place on the 1996 RAC Rally following.

Skoda Motorsport introduced the 2.0-litre, front-wheel drive Octavia Kit Car in 1997, again competing in selected World Championship Rally rounds. This was an interim project undertaken as development for the company's most challenging programme to date, the Skoda Octavia World Rally Car. These new entrants featured four-wheel drive plus a unique, 5-valve-per-cylinder turbocharged engine. In an encouraging WRC debut campaign in 1999, Skoda scored Manufacturers' points in Greece and Britain and, early in 2000, the Safari Rally. The cars added to Skoda's

The stylish Skoda Sport embodied the fifties ideal of a sports racer, though it appeared in 1949, in time to take part in Czechoslovakia's only post-war F1 Grand Prix, on 25 September of that year at the Masaryk Stadium in Brno. Two cars were built, each with an aluminium two-seat body. The more powerful of the duo benefited from a Roots supercharger. (Skoda UK)

Skoda Sports were regular entrants in the Le Mans race. This shows the smaller, 1089 cc, non-supercharged car, driven by Jaroslav Netusil. Over the next couple of years engine capacity was increased, first to 1220, then 1491cc. (Graham Whyte collection)

The exemplary aerodynamic fuselage of the Formula 3 car, and its perfectly balanced profile are captured in this depiction of it competing at the Sachsenring as far back as 1958. The sequence of paintings in this chapter, issued by Skoda's publicity department in the mid-1980s to commemorate the company's long involvement in many aspects of motorsport, are worth including for their atmospheric portrayal of racing and rallying – as well as their rarity value. (Graham Whyte collection)

reputation for durability, finishing nine consecutive rallies between June 1999 and September 2000.

In September 2000 the team introduced a new Octavia WRC. The four-cylinder, 20-valve, turbocharged engine with 300bhp, and torque of 600Nm at 3250rpm is the most powerful engine yet from Skoda Motorsport. In these second-generation Octavia World Rally Cars, drivers Armin Schwarz and Bruno Thiry have already demonstrated their potential by scoring an impressive five points in the first round of the 2001 season, the Monte Carlo Rally. From the early days of motorcycle racing to the latest Octavia WRC, Skoda and motor sport have been synonymous. The strength, reliability and exceptional handling of the cars have given Skoda an enviable record in motor sport for the past 100 years.

At the end of the fifties there were various neat looking Skoda competition and sports cars built, though none entered volume production. This 1100 Coupé was the one that would have lent itself to commercialisation, looking like a cross between a Fairthorpe and a Lotus.

1957's 1100 Type 968 was not designed for polite motoring. Everything about it told of its willingness to mix it with D-Types and Maseratis. (Skoda UK)

This Type 720 Spider, likewise, looks what it is – a classic with a heritage dating back to the golden age of racing. (Skoda UK)

Here it is in its element on the race-track in 1973. (Graham Whyte collection)

The Type 733 was powered by
an 1800cc engine, which took it
to a maximum speed of 150mph,
while racing in the Soviet Union
the same year. (Graham Whyte
collection)

The company was active in all
areas of motorsport – even
buggy racing in Russia, with
this contraption from 1972,
powered by an 1107cc engine.
Designated Type 736, it was
designed by Skoda's apprentice
department. (Graham Whyte
collection)

Skoda's current rally-bred road car is the Octavia RS. The name goes back far enough to have a claim over Ford. This is a 1997cc 200 RS competing in the Skoda Rally in 1974. (Graham Whyte collection)

Skoda's rear-engined cars showed themselves to be every bit as competent on the competition circuit as more traditional models. This 1197cc Type 120 took part in the RAC Rally in 1975. (Graham Whyte collection)

A 1299cc 130 RS during the European Championship race at Brno in 1976. (Graham Whyte collection)

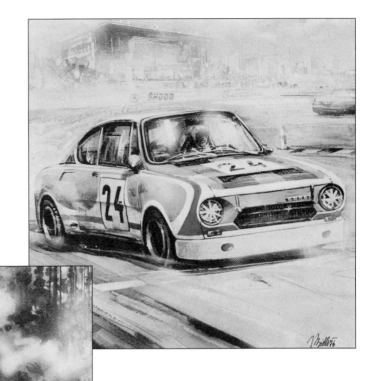

Raising the dust in the 1977 Monte Carlo, this car combined the mechanical bits of the 130 RS with the smooth shape of the 110R and maintained a speed of 100mph. (Graham Whyte collection)

And here it is in the Skoda Museum. (Skoda UK)

John Haugland was a Skoda dealer from Norway, who was also no mean driver. He drove in, and won, a number of events for the firm, such as the Skoda Rally of 1977. (Graham Whyte collection)

The Monte Carlo was also well established on Skoda's victory trail for many years. Here's Blahna driving a 1977 130 RS. Eleven years earlier Keinanen and Vainsilia had beaten a team of three Alfas to victory in the 1300cc class. (Graham Whyte collection)

Zdenek Vojtech was a highly skilled engineer and one of Skoda's leading drivers. Like his colleagues, he suffered extreme frustration from the apathy and red tape inflicted upon them by bureaucratic management. Unlike his colleagues, he voiced his frustration to the press. Despite the team's victory in the European championships in 1980–1, he was called before party officials and disciplined, Here he is in 1980, driving a 130 RS. (Graham Whyte collection)

Michl was another engineer who drove RS Skodas in competition. Here he is in the 1981 European Championships. (Graham Whyte collection)

Thanks to some administrative shenanigans, the main works team for the 1982 European Championships came not from Mlada Boleslav, but from the HQ of the sporting committee. Large sums of money and other incentives had been handed to the preferred team – along with all the technology and design achievements to date of Mlada B. Playing them at their own game, the Skoda team came up with their own car – the 120 LS, driven here by Dolezal. It showed initiative, but was not a great success. (Graham Whyte collection)

Waste not, want not. Here's the Skoda Buggy design, delivered by the apprentices ten years earlier, leading the field in the 1982 European Autocross Championship. (Graham Whyte collection)

Krecek and Motul head up the Russian Championship in 1983 in another, more successful outing for the 120 LS. (Graham Whyte collection)

I don't quite know how to tell you this. What you're looking at in this picture was the solution arrived at when Mlada Boleslav enlisted the army's help in competing with the favoured team of the Sports Council. Called the Skoda Garde, it is powered (titter ye not) by a 1600cc Lada engine. No, please. Don't mock. The thing in the package on the roof, doubling the wind-resistance, must be a giant Weetabix. I don't think it helped. (Graham Whyte collection)

In 1983 homologation for the 130 RS ran out and, with it, luck for the Sports Council's team. They could hone and boost, but they couldn't come up with a car from scratch. Mlada Bolly could and did, in the form of the 130 L. (Graham Whyte collection)

The new Octavia has already proven itself to be more than equal to Skoda's rallying reputation. A hundred years on from the fearless beginnings of Pod, Count Kolowrat and the other pioneering heroes of motoring, there are new challenges brought by ever improving driving standards and ever improving technology. (Skoda UK)

Perhaps the major key to the passionate support for Skoda Motorsport is the fact that it happily coexists on two distinct levels. While the professional works teams squeeze ever more blood from the marque's most recent offerings, amateur enthusiasts the world over meet to race, modify, customise and tweak the simpler, more accessible motors of an earlier period. (Simon Clarke)

The measure of enjoyment to be had from these old cars is bounded only by limitations of the imagination. Clubs not only provide a focus for shared enthusiasm, but bring together skills and equipment needed to maintain and get the most from cars deserving of an 'enhanced entry' in the annals of amateur motorsport. (Simon Clarke)

Regular trips are made by Skoda owners to follow rally events in different parts of the world. The Octavia WRC has succeeded brilliantly in rekindling, maintaining and inspiring new fervour for the company's sporting achievements. (Skoda UK)

Another crucial basis for the affinity between spectators and competitors is the fact that Skoda rally cars are not too far removed from those in the dealers' showrooms. If you've ever driven an Octavia, you can get an idea of what it's like piloting the WRC through ice and dust. (Skoda UK)

Those of us fortunate (and foolhardy) enough to have been whisked around Millbrook by one of Skoda's crack competition drivers can attest to the cars' remarkable roadgoing capabilities – way beyond anything required of them in everyday driving situations – and the feeling of security this engenders when driving them to a fraction of their design limitations. (Peter Grenfell)

'We're waiting for a part, mate. Should have it back together by the weekend.' As much as any other, rallying is a team event, with the Armin Schwartzes of this world depending on armies of designers, engineers, tuning specialists, co-ordinators, transporter drivers and strategists, without any of whom the positive world image of Skoda Motorsport would not be able to maintain its definition. (Peter Grenfell)

The Octavia in which Emil Triner drove to victory in the 1999 Rally of Bohemia. (Peter Grenfell)

Full circle (nearly). Latter day rally ace poses with his own classic Skoda Rapid, neatly symbolising the unbroken line of motoring heroes that began with the likes of Kolowrat and Podsednicek. (Skoda UK)

ACKNOWLEDGEMENTS

The author would like to acknowledge the invaluable assistance provided by the following:

The Skoda UK Press Office, especially Catherine Bell, Eilish O'Shea (now a PR Manager at Volkswagen's International Media Office) – and Juliet Edwards, who helped get the project off the ground and has since moved on to head up the SEAT Press Office.

Simon Clarke and Peter Grenfell from the Skoda Owners' Club for their expert knowledge and enthusiasm, making their cars available and allowing me to raid their photo archives.

Graham Whyte FCIJ, who, in another life, provided support for the Skoda Rally Team, for use of items from his collection.

Peter Cracknell for helping me out from his extensive, and mystifyingly well-organised, photo-archives, and for co-driving and sharing photography on past and (hopefully) future Skoda launches.

Julian Nowill for kindly filling in some gaps with photographs that wouldn't fit in his own book – the comprehensive and indispensable *East European Cars*.

Simon Fletcher for his confidence, enthusiasm and, above all, patience, from the mist-enshrouded beginnings of this project, via the invention of printing, to its fruition as the last in a long and otherwise distinguished line of Sutton's motoring books.

Special thanks are also due to Peter Kožíček and Jan Králík, whose exhaustive researches and incomparable knowledge of local realities and subject matter inform their definitive two-tome official biography of the marque.

Without them, this book would not have been possible.

Thanks also to my wife, Sue, and 'Mdala' Don Bottom, for their assistance in identifying pictures.

INDEX